Last Minute Revision

MATHEMATICS WORKBOOK 5

Useful for Unit Tests, School Examinations & Olympiads

Author
Prasoon Kumar
Peer Reviewer
Jyotsna Gopikrishnan

As per Updated CBSE Pattern

Strictly According to Latest NCERT Syllabus

V&S PUBLISHERS

Published by:

V&S PUBLISHERS

F-2/16, Ansari road, Daryaganj, New Delhi-110002
☎ 23240026, 23240027 • *Fax:* 011-23240028
Email: info@vspublishers.com • *Website:* www.vspublishers.com
Online Brandstore: amazon.in/vspublishers

Regional Office : Hyderabad
5-1-707/1, Brij Bhawan (Beside Central Bank of India Lane)
Bank Street, Koti, Hyderabad - 500 095
☎ 040-24737290
E-mail: vspublishershyd@gmail.com

Branch Office : Mumbai
Jaywant Industrial Estate, 1st Floor–108, Tardeo Road
Opposite Sobo Central Mall, Mumbai – 400 034
☎ 022-23510736
E-mail: vspublishersmum@gmail.com

BUY OUR BOOKS FROM: AMAZON FLIPKART

ISBN 978-93-579424-8-5
Edition 2020

DISCLAIMER

Publisher's Note

The current decade has firmly established V&S Publishers as one of the leading publishers of general trade mass appeal books across popular genres in India. With over 800 titles available in print and digital versions, we cater to readers worldwide via popular e-commerce platforms, booksellers and chain stores. We serve people from all strata of society by publishing books that are informative yet affordable. Our primary categories are Self-help, Student Development, Children, Health and Language Learning.

Keeping pace with emerging trends and market demands, we stepped into long-felt searching need to publish academic books. We, at V&S Publishers, felt that there was a need to publish student-centric books, which are presented in a unique manner. This realization led us into creating books that had content put together imaginatively yet serving the same purpose of preparing students for various exams.

Based on this ideology, our series of Olympiad titles (including a proprietary online version for Olympiad test preparation) from class 1 to 10 in the subjects of Science, Mathematics, Computers and English have revolutionized the way books are written and have rightfully received outstanding response from students and parents alike. The sale of each title, as reported by booksellers, remains the high watermark in annals of Olympiad examination preparatory books.

Encouraged further by the wide acceptability of our Olympiad series, we decided to enlarge our sphere of activity by publishing Workbooks – developed to help students become exam-ready. The books currently being published are on the subjects Science, Mathematics, Computer, Social Science, English, Hindi and General Knowledge. You can treat this book as a part of Last Minute Revision series, which has been written keeping in mind how students actually prepare for various exams. The students, in order to score high, resort to unethical methods like cramming & cheating besides undergoing stressful eye-burning studies, which often leads to them faltering in the exam. This series of books is our way of helping students do a last-minute revision just before the exam.

Unlike other run-of-the-mill published Workbooks that are just about stereotypes replicating the Long answer, Short answer, Multiple choice questions etc. from a chosen chapter and surreptitiously selling as guide books, our series covers the same chapter but in a holistically wider manner. These Workbooks are written as per NCERT syllabi and comprises key concepts and MCQs and have been prepared with updated syllabus-precision so that any student who ticks (darkens the circle) 80-90% correct answers in the OMR sheet can expect to do well in the exams. Note that important concepts in point-wise format have also been summarised in the beginning of the chapter for ease in revision. This will help the student not only to discuss the subject across the class confidently, but also to score high in all Unit tests, school exams and Semester papers. Moreover, going through a workbook immediately prior to exam will just be a matter of few hours. We are positive that this novel initiative by V&S Publishers' editorial team will help students prepare well without any stress.

We wish you the best!

P.S. If you come across any error, howsoever minor, anywhere in the book, do not hesitate to discuss with your teachers while pointing that out to us in no uncertain terms. V&S Publishers does not advocate the idea of end-moment studies and advises students to prepare and study on a daily basis. These books are written with a clear objective of final revisions only.

Contents

WORKBOOK

1 Number Sense

- The number system that we use in our everyday life is called decimal system.
- There are 10 digits, namely 0, 1, 2, 3, 4, 5, 6, 7, 8, 9
- The counting numbers are called natural numbers.
  Example : 1, 2, 3, 4, 5, ...
- The natural numbers along with zero are called whole numbers.
  Example : 0, 1, 2, 3, ...
- Negative of natural numbers, zero and positive natural numbers are called integers.
  Example : – 3, – 2, – 1, 0, 1, 2, 3, ...
- A number which is divisible by 2 is called even number.
  Example : 2, 4, 6, 8, ...
- A number which is not divisible by 2 is called odd number.
  Example : 3, 5, 7, ...
- The numbers that have only two factors namely unity and the number itself are called prime number.
  Example : 2, 3, 5, 7, 11, 13, ...
- Composite numbers are the numbers which have other factors beside itself and unity.
  Example : 36, 42, 52, ...
- Numerals can be written by using different symbols. The numeral formed by the digits 0, 1, 2, 3, 4, 5, 6, 7, 8, 9 are known as Hindu Arabic numbers.
- The symbols 0, 1, 2, 3, 4, 5, 6, 7, 8, 9 are called face value of numbers.
- Place value of a digit depends on its position in the number. As the digit moves to left, its value increases.
  Example :

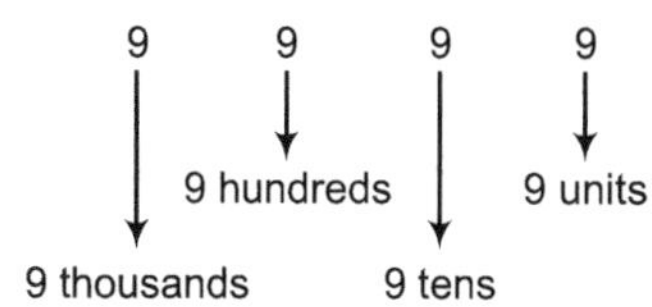

  Example : What is the face value and place value of 5 in 62547?

  Face value = 5

  Place value = 500
- **Comparison of Numbers :** If a number has more digits than the other, then it is the greater of the two.
  Example : 8542 > 941

- If two numbers have the same number of digits, then the number with bigger digit on the extreme left is greater.

  Example : 7592 > 5972
- If two numbers have the same number of digits and the extreme left digits are also same, then compare the next digit to the right and so on.

  Example : 8347 > 8152

Roman Numbers

Roman numerals originated in the ancient Roman empire and are still in use in a variety of forms today.

Roman Numerals

1	I	25	XXV
2	II	30	XXX
3	III	40	XL
4	IV	50	L
5	V	51	LI
6	VI	55	LV
7	VII	90	XC
8	VIII	100	C
9	IX	500	D
10	X	1000	M
20	XX		

Rules for Writing Roman Numerals

- **Rule 1 :** Read from left to right, larger values to the left and work to the smaller values on the right.
- **Rule 2 :** If a lesser symbol is before a greater symbol, the lesser is subtracted from the greater.

  Example : IV = 5 – 1 = 4
- **Rule 3 :** If a lesser symbol is after a greater symbol, the two values are added.

  Example : VI = 5 + 1 = 6
- **Rule 4 :** If a symbol is repeated twice or thrice, the value of the numeral is obtained by adding the value of the symbol as many times it repeats.

  Example : III = 1 + 1 + 1 = 3; XXX = 10 + 10 + 10 = 30
- **Rule 5 :** I and V can only modify upto X. Example : 40 is not written IL rather you first write 40 as XL and then resolve 9 as IX.

  49 = XLIX
- **Rute 6 :** X and L can only modify up to C.

  Example : 490 is not written as XD. First you resolve 400 as CD and resolve 90 as XC.

  490 = CDXC
- **Rule 7 :** C and D can only modify upto M

  950 = CML
- **Rule 8 :** No symbol can be repeated more than thrice.
- **Rule 9 :** To represent larger numbers, a bar is put on the numeral, which means to multiply the number by 1000.

  Example : $\overline{\text{D}}$ represents 1000 × 500 = 500000

Multiple Choice Questions

1. Which of the following is a prime number?
   (a) 57 (b) 67
   (c) 77 (d) 87
2. Which of the following is not a prime number?
   (a) 59 (b) 73
   (c) 89 (d) 91
3. The sum of two even numbers is always _____.
   (a) Even (b) Odd
   (c) Prime (d) None of these
4. Which of the following is an even number?
   (a) 6032 (b) 1079
   (c) 1753 (d) 1987
5. Which of the following is an odd number?
   (a) 179 (b) 294
   (c) 386 (d) 982
6. Which of the following is a prime number?
   (a) 17 (b) 21
   (c) 27 (d) 39
7. Which of the following is the smallest prime number?
   (a) 1 (b) 2
   (c) 3 (d) 5
8. Which of the following is not a prime number?
   (a) 73 (b) 85
   (c) 97 (d) 43
9. What is the predecessor of 809?
   (a) 810 (b) 808
   (c) 807 (d) None of these
10. What is the successor of 999?
    (a) 998 (b) 997
    (c) 1000 (d) 1001
11. What is the sum of the largest 3-digit number and the smallest 3-digit number?
    (a) 1999 (b) 1079
    (c) 1089 (d) 1099
12. What is the face value of 7 in 37658?
    (a) 7 (b) 7000
    (c) 700 (d) None of these
13. The number 24 can be written as a product of prime factors. Which of the following is correct?
    (a) $24 = 3 \times 8$ (b) $24 = 4 \times 6$
    (c) $24 = 2 \times 3 \times 4$ (d) $24 = 2 \times 2 \times 2 \times 3$
14. Which of the following is a composite number?
    (a) 101 (b) 103
    (c) 107 (d) 108
15. Which of the following is not a composite number?
    (a) 102 (b) 105
    (c) 107 (d) 108
16. Which of the following is a composite number?
    (a) 67 (b) 69
    (c) 71 (d) 73
17. Which of the following is not a composite number?
    (a) 97 (b) 99
    (c) 102 (d) 110
18. The place value of 7 in 980756 is _____.
    (a) Seven ones (b) Seven tens
    (c) Seven hundreds (d) Seven thousands
19. What is the difference between the face value and place value of 5 in 76523?
    (a) 495 (b) 505
    (c) 45 (d) 5
20. What is the sum of the greatest number and the smallest number of three digits made by the digits 3, 2, 7?
    (a) 969 (b) 996
    (c) 960 (d) None of these

21. What is the difference of the largest number and the smallest number of three digits made by the digits 5, 7, 9 if repetition of number is not allowed?
   (a) 378 (b) 396
   (c) 216 (d) None of these
22. Which of the following symbols is used for 30975 □ 39075?
   (a) > (b) <
   (c) = (d) None of these
23. What is the sum of prime numbers that lies between 50 and 70?
   (a) 237 (b) 238
   (c) 240 (d) None of these
24. What is the sum of all the prime numbers from 1 to 30?
   (a) 128 (b) 126
   (c) 127 (d) 129
25. What must be added to 897 to get the greatest three digit number?
   (a) 112 (b) 102
   (c) 92 (d) 122
26. What must be subtracted from the greatest three digit number to get a result of 563?
   (a) 336 (b) 536
   (c) 436 (d) 476
27. The number 2197 is expressed in expanded form. Which of the following is correct?
   (a) 2000 + 100 + 90 + 7
   (b) 2000 + 197
   (c) 2100 + 97
   (d) 2190 + 7
28. Which of the following is correct?
   (a) Every natural number is a whole number
   (b) Every whole number is a natural number
   (c) Every integer is a whole number
   (d) Every rational number is a whole number
29. Which of the following is a correct sequence of numbers in ascending order?
   (a) 497, 463, 527, 597
   (b) 369, 453, 397, 602, 429
   (c) 409, 476, 503, 598, 617
   (d) 375, 604, 568, 762, 464
30. Which of the following is a correct sequence of numbers in descending order?
   (a) 568, 674, 402, 613, 779
   (b) 324, 574, 623, 709, 854
   (c) 902, 873, 767, 725, 526
   (d) 297, 843, 564, 794, 478
31. Which of the following is divisible by 5?
   (a) 625 (b) 307
   (c) 462 (d) 764
32. Which of the following is not divisible by 2?
   (a) 562 (b) 784
   (c) 860 (d) 791
33. Which of the following is a perfect square?
   (a) 72 (b) 64
   (c) 48 (d) 96
34. Which of the following is not a perfect square?
   (a) 49 (b) 64
   (c) 86 (d) 81
35. What is the difference between the smallest and the largest 4-digit number made by the digits 7, 0, 8, 6 if repetition of digits is not allowed?
   (a) 2682 (b) 2782
   (c) 2862 (d) 2762
36. The Roman numeral CXII is equal to ______.
   (a) 109 (b) 110
   (c) 111 (d) 112
37. The Roman numeral LXXXIV is equal to ______.
   (a) 74 (b) 84
   (c) 94 (d) 104
38. The Roman numeral XLIV is equal to ______.
   (a) 44 (b) 114
   (c) 147 (d) 128

39. The correct Roman numeral that represents 40 is ________.
    (a) XL (b) XXXX
    (c) XLC (d) None of these

40. Which of the following is the correct Roman numeral for 3396?
    (a) MMMCCCXCVI (b) MMMCXCVI
    (c) MDCXXXVI (d) None of these

41. Which alphabet represents 1000 in Roman numeral?
    (a) M (b) D
    (c) C (d) L

42. The Roman numeral $\overline{V}$ represents ________.
    (a) 1000 (b) 5000
    (c) 10,000 (d) 50,000

43. Which of the following Roman numeral represents 50,000?
    (a) $\overline{L}$ (b) $\overline{M}$
    (c) $\overline{D}$ (d) $\overline{X}$

44. What is the Roman numeral equivalent of 12391?
    (a) $\overline{X}$MMCCCXCI
    (b) $\overline{X}$MMMCCXCI
    (c) $\overline{X}$MMCCCCXCI
    (d) None of these

45. Which of the following is the correct Roman numeral for 5074?
    (a) $\overline{V}$LXXXIV (b) $\overline{V}$LXXIV
    (c) $\overline{V}$LXXCIV (d) $\overline{V}$LCXIV

46. Which of the following Roman numeral represents 1266?
    (a) MCCLXVI (b) MCCLLXVI
    (c) MCCLXV (d) None of these

47. What is the equivalent of MMMCCXXIV?
    (a) 3224 (b) 3324
    (c) 3124 (d) None of these

48. What is equivalent to MMCIV?
    (a) 2104 (b) 2014
    (c) 2214 (d) None of these

49. The Roman numeral MCXI is equal to ______.
    (a) 1011 (b) 1111
    (c) 1101 (d) 1110

50. The Roman numeral $\overline{D}$ represents ______.
    (a) 5000 (b) 50,000
    (c) 500000 (d) None of these

☺☺☺

Darken Your Choice with HB Pencil

1.	ⓐ	ⓑ	ⓒ	ⓓ	11.	ⓐ	ⓑ	ⓒ	ⓓ	21.	ⓐ	ⓑ	ⓒ	ⓓ	31.	ⓐ	ⓑ	ⓒ	ⓓ	41.	ⓐ	ⓑ	ⓒ	ⓓ
2.	ⓐ	ⓑ	ⓒ	ⓓ	12.	ⓐ	ⓑ	ⓒ	ⓓ	22.	ⓐ	ⓑ	ⓒ	ⓓ	32.	ⓐ	ⓑ	ⓒ	ⓓ	42.	ⓐ	ⓑ	ⓒ	ⓓ
3.	ⓐ	ⓑ	ⓒ	ⓓ	13.	ⓐ	ⓑ	ⓒ	ⓓ	23.	ⓐ	ⓑ	ⓒ	ⓓ	33.	ⓐ	ⓑ	ⓒ	ⓓ	43.	ⓐ	ⓑ	ⓒ	ⓓ
4.	ⓐ	ⓑ	ⓒ	ⓓ	14.	ⓐ	ⓑ	ⓒ	ⓓ	24.	ⓐ	ⓑ	ⓒ	ⓓ	34.	ⓐ	ⓑ	ⓒ	ⓓ	44.	ⓐ	ⓑ	ⓒ	ⓓ
5.	ⓐ	ⓑ	ⓒ	ⓓ	15.	ⓐ	ⓑ	ⓒ	ⓓ	25.	ⓐ	ⓑ	ⓒ	ⓓ	35.	ⓐ	ⓑ	ⓒ	ⓓ	45.	ⓐ	ⓑ	ⓒ	ⓓ
6.	ⓐ	ⓑ	ⓒ	ⓓ	16.	ⓐ	ⓑ	ⓒ	ⓓ	26.	ⓐ	ⓑ	ⓒ	ⓓ	36.	ⓐ	ⓑ	ⓒ	ⓓ	46.	ⓐ	ⓑ	ⓒ	ⓓ
7.	ⓐ	ⓑ	ⓒ	ⓓ	17.	ⓐ	ⓑ	ⓒ	ⓓ	27.	ⓐ	ⓑ	ⓒ	ⓓ	37.	ⓐ	ⓑ	ⓒ	ⓓ	47.	ⓐ	ⓑ	ⓒ	ⓓ
8.	ⓐ	ⓑ	ⓒ	ⓓ	18.	ⓐ	ⓑ	ⓒ	ⓓ	28.	ⓐ	ⓑ	ⓒ	ⓓ	38.	ⓐ	ⓑ	ⓒ	ⓓ	48.	ⓐ	ⓑ	ⓒ	ⓓ
9.	ⓐ	ⓑ	ⓒ	ⓓ	19.	ⓐ	ⓑ	ⓒ	ⓓ	29.	ⓐ	ⓑ	ⓒ	ⓓ	39.	ⓐ	ⓑ	ⓒ	ⓓ	49.	ⓐ	ⓑ	ⓒ	ⓓ
10.	ⓐ	ⓑ	ⓒ	ⓓ	20.	ⓐ	ⓑ	ⓒ	ⓓ	30.	ⓐ	ⓑ	ⓒ	ⓓ	40.	ⓐ	ⓑ	ⓒ	ⓓ	50.	ⓐ	ⓑ	ⓒ	ⓓ

WORKBOOK

2 Operations on Numbers

- **Addition :** In this operation, two or more numbers are added.

  Example : Add 3473, 2972 and 5476

$$\begin{array}{r} 3473 \\ 2972 \\ +5476 \\ \hline 11921 \\ \hline \end{array}$$

- **Properties of Addition :** When we change the order of numbers, the sum remains the same.

$$13 + 12 = 12 + 13 = 25$$

- When we add 0 to any number, the sum is the number itself.

$$25 + 0 = 25, 0 + 17 = 17$$

- **Subtraction :** In this operation, difference between two numbers is found.

  Example : Subtract 4072 from 5123?

$$\begin{array}{r} 5123 \\ -4072 \\ \hline 1051 \\ \hline \end{array}$$

- **Properties of Subtraction :**

  When zero is subtracted from any number, the difference is the number itself.

$$49 - 0 = 49, \qquad 35 - 0 = 35$$

- **Multiplication :** The number to be multiplied is called multiplicand. The number by which we multiply is the multiplier.

  Example : Multiply 357 with 413

$$\begin{array}{r} 357 \\ 413 \\ \hline 1071 \\ 357\times \\ 1428\times\times \\ \hline 147441 \\ \hline \end{array}$$

- **Properties of Multiplication**

  Any number multiplied by 1 is the number itself.

$$17 \times 1 = 17$$

- Any number multiplied by zero is always 0.
- The product of numbers remains same even after changing their order.

$$35 \times 17 = 17 \times 35$$

- **Division :** It is the opposite of multiplication. When any number is divided by 1, the quotient is the number itself.

BODMAS Rule

Order	Abbreviated letter used in rule	Meaning	Notation
1	B	Bracket	[ ], { }, ( )
2	O	Of	Of
3	D	Division	÷
4	M	Multiplication	×
5	A	Addition	+
6	S	Subtraction	–

Example 1 : $12 - 16 \div 4 + 3 \text{ of } 7 - (2 + 5)$

$= 12 - 16 \div 4 + 3 \text{ of } 7 - 7$

$= 12 - 16 \div 4 + 21 - 7$

$= 12 - 4 + 21 - 7$

$= 33 - 11$

$= 22$

Example 2 : $17 - 32 \div 4 \times 2 + 5$

$= 17 - 8 \times 2 + 5$

$= 17 - 16 + 5$

$= 22 - 16$

$= 6$

Multiple Choice Questions

1. Find the dividend when divisor is 257, quotient is 307 and the remainder is 73.
   (a) 78792 (b) 78972
   (c) 78672 (d) 78872
2. What is the quotient if dividend is 2049, divisor is 179 and remainder is 80?
   (a) 9 (b) 10
   (c) 11 (d) 12
3. What number must be added to the sum of 4567 and 2978 to get the largest four digit number?
   (a) 2354 (b) 2454
   (c) 2554 (d) 2494
4. What is the difference between the largest five digit number and the smallest five digit number?
   (a) 81,999 (b) 89,999
   (c) 80,999 (d) 88,999
5. What is the sum of the smallest four digit number and the largest three digit number?
   (a) 1799 (b) 1899
   (c) 1999 (d) None of these
6. The total population of a city is 5,03,709. If the number of male members is 2,79,447, then what is the number of female members?
   (a) 224262 (b) 242262
   (c) 224242 (d) 224282
7. The total number of students in class V in a state is 6723679. Of these 3697736 are girls. How many boys are there?
   (a) 3205943 (b) 3025943
   (c) 3029543 (d) 3025963
8. A poultry farm produces 2540160 eggs and packs 144 eggs in a box. How many boxes are required to pack all the eggs?
   (a) 16780 (b) 16740
   (c) 17620 (d) 17640
9. A building has 36 flats. Each flat has four rooms. Each room requires 172 floor tiles. How many tiles would be required for the building?
   (a) 24748 (b) 24768
   (c) 24868 (d) 24788
10. What will be the quotient if the greatest number of 9 digits is divided by the greatest number of 3 digits?
    (a) 1001001 (b) 1001011
    (c) 1000001 (d) 1001101
11. What will be the remainder when the greatest number of three digits is divided by the smallest number of two digits?
    (a) 7 (b) 8
    (c) 9 (d) None of these
12. A factory produces 13078 bulbs per day. How many bulbs can be produced in 178 days?
    (a) 2327284 (b) 2327864
    (c) 2327484 (d) 2327884
13. A train covers 72 kilometers in one hour. How much distance will it cover in 17 hours?
    (a) 1024 km (b) 1124 km
    (c) 1224 km (d) 1324 km
14. 547 sweets have to be distributed equally among 18 boys. How many sweets are left after distribution?
    (a) 3 (b) 5
    (c) 6 (d) 7
15. The difference of two numbers is 137907 and the smaller number is 837623. What is the larger number?
    (a) 975520 (b) 957530
    (c) 985530 (d) 975530
16. The difference of two numbers is 403127 and the larger number is 960374. What is the smaller number?
    (a) 557247 (b) 557257
    (c) 537247 (d) 547247

17. The product of two numbers is 391608. If one number is 444, then what is the other number?
(a) 882 (b) 872
(c) 892 (d) 792

18. The product of two numbers is 153468. If one of them is 882, then what is the other number?
(a) 174 (b) 184
(c) 194 (d) 214

19. In a garden there are 73 rows of trees. In each row there are 47 trees. How many trees are there in the garden?
(a) 3441 (b) 3431
(c) 3451 (d) 3471

20. There are 893 pages in an English dictionary. Each page contains 39 words. What is the total number of words in that dictionary?
(a) 34847 (b) 34837
(c) 33827 (d) 34827

21. If 72 persons can seat in a rail coach. How many such coaches are required to seat 4032 persons?
(a) 46 (b) 56
(c) 66 (d) 76

22. What is the value of $(3 + 4)^2 - 5 \times 3 + 3^2$?
(a) 41 (b) 42
(c) 43 (d) 44

23. What is the value of
$(27 \div 3 + 4) - (2^3 - 2 \times 7)$?
(a) 19 (b) 17
(c) 15 (d) 21

24. What is the value of
$(4^3 \div 8 + 7) - (3^2 - 7 \times 2)$?
(a) 20 (b) 21
(c) 22 (d) 24

25. What is the value of
$(7^3 - 2 \times 13) + (5 \times 7 - 2^3)$?
(a) 341 (b) 342
(c) 343 (d) 344

26. What is the value of
$5 + 7 \times 2 - 32 \div 4$?
(a) 7 (b) 8
(c) 9 (d) 11

27. What is the value of $71 - 24 - 75 \div 15 + 17$?
(a) 56 (b) 57
(c) 59 (d) 60

28. What is the value of $4^3 + 19 \times 3 - 67$?
(a) 53 (b) 54
(c) 56 (d) 58

29. What is the value of $17 \times 2 + 7 - 175 \div 7$?
(a) 13 (b) 14
(c) 15 (d) 16

30. What is the value of $52 - 4^3 + (8 \times 17) \div 4$?
(a) 22 (b) 23
(c) 24 (d) 26

31. In a basket, there are 123 apples, 96 oranges and 239 mangoes. Out of these 17 mangoes, 13 oranges and 47 apples are damaged. How many fresh fruits are there in the basket?
(a) 361 (b) 371
(c) 381 (d) 391

32. In a herd there are 407 oxen, 364 cows, 293 goats and 417 sheeps. What is the total number of cattles in the herd?
(a) 1281 (b) 1381
(c) 1461 (d) 1481

33. There are 967 pages in a book. Mohan reads 263 pages on Sunday and 497 pages on Monday. How many pages are left to read?
(a) 307 (b) 207
(c) 217 (d) 237

34. What is the quotient if the largest number of six digits is divided by 777?
(a) 1187 (b) 1237
(c) 1257 (d) 1287

35. What is the dividend if divisor is 269, quotient is 107 and remainder is 57?
(a) 28840 (b) 28480
(c) 28860 (d) None of these

36. The cost of 5 shirts is 3745. How many such shirts can be bought for ₹ 71155?
(a) 75 (b) 85
(c) 95 (d) 97

37. What is obtained when 67 lakhs 5 thousand ninety seven is subtracted from one crore?
(a) 3394903 (b) 3294903
(c) 3296803 (d) 3295803

38. Simplify 23097 + 67309 – 47368 ?
(a) 43308 (b) 43038
(c) 43048 (d) 43068

39. Simplify 765938 – 892097 + 460353
(a) 334294 (b) 334194
(c) 334394 (d) None of these

40. What is the difference between face value and place value of 6 in the number 856973?
(a) 6973 (b) 5994
(c) 5996 (d) 973

41. 8597 – ? = 7429 – 4358
(a) 5476 (b) 5426
(c) 5526 (d) 5726

42. 3251 + 587 + ? – 1200 = 3007
(a) 369 (b) 379
(c) 359 (d) 349

43. $976 \times 237 + 976 \times 763 = ?$
(a) 926000 (b) 956000
(c) 976000 (d) None of these

44. Replace * with the correct digit·

$$\begin{array}{r} 900427 \\ -\ 76{*}586 \\ \hline 131841 \\ \hline \end{array}$$

(a) 6 (b) 7
(c) 8 (d) 9

45. Replace * with the correct digit ________.

$$\begin{array}{r} 759684 \\ +\ 86{*}397 \\ \hline 1627081 \\ \hline \end{array}$$

(a) 5 (b) 6
(c) 7 (d) 8

46. What is the quotient when 806873 is divided by 637 and leaves the remainder 431?
(a) 1261 (b) 1263
(c) 1266 (d) 1267

47. Which of the following expression evaluates 17?
(a) $6 + 5 \times 3 - 8$ (b) $7 + 5 \times 3 - 5$
(c) $5 + 4 \times 3 - 3$ (d) $3 + 5 + 5 - 5$

48. Evaluate $7 + 16 \div 4 - (3 + 5) + 2 \times 3$.
(a) 7 (b) 9
(c) 6 (d) 12

49. Evaluate $29 - 32 \div 8 + (5 - 7) + 8$·
(a) 31 (b) 33
(c) 15 (d) 17

50. Evaluate $17 - 3^3 + 5 - 2(4 - 7)$ ·
(a) 1 (b) 2
(c) 3 (d) 6

Darken Your Choice with HB Pencil

1.	ⓐ	ⓑ	ⓒ	ⓓ	11.	ⓐ	ⓑ	ⓒ	ⓓ	21.	ⓐ	ⓑ	ⓒ	ⓓ	31.	ⓐ	ⓑ	ⓒ	ⓓ	41.	ⓐ	ⓑ	ⓒ	ⓓ
2.	ⓐ	ⓑ	ⓒ	ⓓ	12.	ⓐ	ⓑ	ⓒ	ⓓ	22.	ⓐ	ⓑ	ⓒ	ⓓ	32.	ⓐ	ⓑ	ⓒ	ⓓ	42.	ⓐ	ⓑ	ⓒ	ⓓ
3.	ⓐ	ⓑ	ⓒ	ⓓ	13.	ⓐ	ⓑ	ⓒ	ⓓ	23.	ⓐ	ⓑ	ⓒ	ⓓ	33.	ⓐ	ⓑ	ⓒ	ⓓ	43.	ⓐ	ⓑ	ⓒ	ⓓ
4.	ⓐ	ⓑ	ⓒ	ⓓ	14.	ⓐ	ⓑ	ⓒ	ⓓ	24.	ⓐ	ⓑ	ⓒ	ⓓ	34.	ⓐ	ⓑ	ⓒ	ⓓ	44.	ⓐ	ⓑ	ⓒ	ⓓ
5.	ⓐ	ⓑ	ⓒ	ⓓ	15.	ⓐ	ⓑ	ⓒ	ⓓ	25.	ⓐ	ⓑ	ⓒ	ⓓ	35.	ⓐ	ⓑ	ⓒ	ⓓ	45.	ⓐ	ⓑ	ⓒ	ⓓ
6.	ⓐ	ⓑ	ⓒ	ⓓ	16.	ⓐ	ⓑ	ⓒ	ⓓ	26.	ⓐ	ⓑ	ⓒ	ⓓ	36.	ⓐ	ⓑ	ⓒ	ⓓ	46.	ⓐ	ⓑ	ⓒ	ⓓ
7.	ⓐ	ⓑ	ⓒ	ⓓ	17.	ⓐ	ⓑ	ⓒ	ⓓ	27.	ⓐ	ⓑ	ⓒ	ⓓ	37.	ⓐ	ⓑ	ⓒ	ⓓ	47.	ⓐ	ⓑ	ⓒ	ⓓ
8.	ⓐ	ⓑ	ⓒ	ⓓ	18.	ⓐ	ⓑ	ⓒ	ⓓ	28.	ⓐ	ⓑ	ⓒ	ⓓ	38.	ⓐ	ⓑ	ⓒ	ⓓ	48.	ⓐ	ⓑ	ⓒ	ⓓ
9.	ⓐ	ⓑ	ⓒ	ⓓ	19.	ⓐ	ⓑ	ⓒ	ⓓ	29.	ⓐ	ⓑ	ⓒ	ⓓ	39.	ⓐ	ⓑ	ⓒ	ⓓ	49.	ⓐ	ⓑ	ⓒ	ⓓ
10.	ⓐ	ⓑ	ⓒ	ⓓ	20.	ⓐ	ⓑ	ⓒ	ⓓ	30.	ⓐ	ⓑ	ⓒ	ⓓ	40.	ⓐ	ⓑ	ⓒ	ⓓ	50.	ⓐ	ⓑ	ⓒ	ⓓ

WORKBOOK 3

Decimals and Fractions

- Decimal point is used to separate whole number part from fractional part.
- In 57.46, 57 is a whole number part and 46 is fractional part.

  It can be expressed as

$$57.46 = 5 \times 10 + 7 \times 1 + 4 \times \frac{1}{10} + 6 \times \frac{1}{100}$$

- **Adding and Subtracting Decimals**

  Example : Add 12.357 and 15.709

$$\begin{array}{r} 12.357 \\ +\ 15.709 \\ \hline 28.066 \\ \hline \end{array}$$

Example : Subtract 42.907 from 51

$$\begin{array}{r} 51.000 \\ -\ 42.907 \\ \hline 8.093 \\ \hline \end{array}$$

- **Multiplication of Decimals**

  Example : Multiply 3.46 to 0.05

$$\begin{array}{r} 346 \\ \times\ 5 \\ \hline 1730 \\ \hline \end{array}$$

$$3.46 \times 0.05 = 0.1730 = 0.173$$

Fraction is a part of whole.

$$\text{Fraction} = \frac{\text{Numerator}}{\text{Denominator}}$$

Example : $\frac{3}{5}, \frac{7}{5}$ are fractions.

- **Equivalent Fraction :**

$$\frac{2}{3}=\frac{4}{6}=\frac{6}{9}=\frac{8}{12}$$

In this example $\frac{4}{6}, \frac{6}{9}$ and $\frac{8}{12}$ are equivalent fractions of $\frac{2}{3}$.

- **Convert fractions into decimals**

Example : $\frac{4}{5}=\frac{4 \times 20}{5 \times 20}=\frac{80}{100}=0.8$

Example : $\frac{3}{25}=\frac{3 \times 4}{25 \times 4}=\frac{12}{100}=0.12$

- **Convert decimals into fractions**

Example : $15.67=\frac{1567}{100}=15\frac{67}{100}$

$2.3=2\frac{3}{10}$

$0.46=\frac{46}{100}=\frac{23}{50}$

Multiple Choice Questions

1. The number 6784 expressed to the nearest hundred is _____.
   (a) 6700 (b) 6780
   (c) 6790 (d) 6800
2. Which of the following is the smallest fraction?
   (a) $\frac{4}{5}$ (b) $\frac{3}{7}$ (c) $\frac{5}{6}$ (d) $\frac{2}{7}$
3. Which of the following is the largest fraction?
   (a) $\frac{5}{8}$ (b) $\frac{6}{7}$
   (c) $\frac{7}{9}$ (d) $\frac{8}{11}$
4. Which of the following is the smallest decimal number?
   (a) 0.6245 (b) 0.2698
   (c) 0.0987 (d) 0.9201
5. Which of the following is the largest decimal number?
   (a) 0.6027 (b) 0.6139
   (c) 0.6209 (d) 0.6932
6. What is the result if 7.627 is subtracted from 9?
   (a) 2.323 (b) 1.373
   (c) 2.373 (d) 3.173
7. What is the sum of 4.638 and 9.702?
   (a) 14.34 (b) 13.34
   (c) 13.74 (d) 13.94
8. What is the difference between 3.026 and 3.107 ?
   (a) 0.81 (b) 0.081
   (c) 0.801 (d) 0.018
9. Which of the following can be written in the box?
   $$\frac{7}{2} = \frac{\square}{14}$$
   (a) 46 (b) 47
   (c) 49 (d) 48
10. Which of the following can be written in the box?
    $$\frac{5}{12} \quad \frac{15}{\square}$$
    (a) 32 (b) 36
    (c) 38 (d) 42
11. Which of the following is an equivalent fraction of $\frac{3}{7}$?
    (a) $\frac{9}{21}$ (b) $\frac{6}{21}$
    (c) $\frac{12}{21}$ (d) $\frac{15}{28}$
12. Which of the following fractions is not equivalent to $\frac{2}{5}$?
    (a) $\frac{6}{15}$ (b) $\frac{10}{25}$
    (c) $\frac{8}{25}$ (d) $\frac{14}{35}$
13. Which of the following is obtained when $\frac{6}{25}$ is expressed in decimal?
    (a) 0.18 (b) 0.23
    (c) 0.24 (d) 0.25
14. The simplest form of $\frac{42}{60}$ is _______.
    (a) $\frac{21}{30}$ (b) $\frac{7}{10}$
    (c) $\frac{14}{30}$ (d) $\frac{7}{8}$
15. The equivalent fraction of 0.05 is _______.
    (a) $\frac{1}{20}$ (b) $\frac{1}{2}$
    (c) $\frac{1}{4}$ (d) $\frac{1}{40}$

16. The equivalent decimal of $\frac{8}{35}$ upto four decimal places is ______.
(a) 0.2286 (b) 0.2283
(c) 0.2287 (d) 0.2284

17. What is the sum of 0.0629 and 0.6029?
(a) 0.6658 (b) 0.6648
(c) 0.6638 (d) 0.6628

18. What is the difference between 5.0629 and 5.6401?
(a) 0.5272 (b) 0.5772
(c) 0.6772 (d) None of these

19. If $\frac{1}{4}$ of a number is 28, what is $\frac{1}{2}$ of that number?
(a) 48 (b) 56
(c) 62 (d) 64

20. What is the place value of 7 in the number 36.2375?
(a) 7 tenths (b) 7 hundredths
(c) 7 thousandths (d) None of these

21. If $\frac{1}{8}$ of a number is 27, then what is $\frac{2}{3}$ of that number?
(a) 112 (b) 124
(c) 136 (d) 144

22. What is the value of $1 + 0.1 + 0.01 + 0.001$?
(a) 1.001 (b) 1.011
(c) 1.003 (d) 1.111

23. What is the value of $2.3 + 1.232 + 3.12 + 2.123$?
(a) 8.775 (b) 8.575
(c) 8.565 (d) None of these

24. What is the value of $5.25 + 7.57 - 6.85$?
(a) 5.67 (b) 5.87
(c) 5.97 (d) 5.37

25. What is the value of $\frac{4}{7}+\frac{1}{7}-\frac{2}{7}$?
(a) $\frac{2}{7}$ (b) $\frac{3}{7}$
(c) $\frac{1}{7}$ (d) $\frac{5}{7}$

26. What is the value of 0.4×0.004?
(a) 0.016 (b) 0.0016
(c) 0.16 (d) None of these

27. What is the simplest form of $\frac{35}{245}$?
(a) $\frac{1}{7}$ (b) $\frac{1}{5}$
(c) $\frac{1}{9}$ (d) $\frac{2}{7}$

28. Which of the following is equivalent to 0.003?
(a) $\frac{3}{10}$ (b) $\frac{3}{100}$
(c) $\frac{3}{1000}$ (d) None of these

29. Which of the following is the decimal equivalent of $\frac{3}{4}$?
(a) 0.75 (b) 0.075
(c) 0.65 (d) None of these

30. Which of the following fractions is a like fraction of $\frac{7}{13}$?
(a) $\frac{2}{13}$ (b) $\frac{3}{7}$
(c) $\frac{5}{6}$ (d) $\frac{3}{8}$

31. Which of the following is a proper fraction?
(a) $\frac{5}{6}$ (b) $\frac{7}{3}$
(c) $\frac{5}{2}$ (d) $\frac{11}{7}$

32. Which of the following is an improper fraction?

(a) $\frac{2}{3}$ (b) $\frac{4}{5}$

(c) $\frac{6}{7}$ (d) $\frac{7}{3}$

33. What fraction has denominator 49 and equivalent to $\frac{2}{7}$?

(a) $\frac{14}{49}$ (b) $\frac{21}{49}$

(c) $\frac{12}{49}$ (d) $\frac{17}{49}$

34. The equivalent fraction of $\frac{3}{5}$ with denominator 35 is ______.

(a) $\frac{9}{35}$ (b) $\frac{7}{35}$

(c) $\frac{21}{35}$ (d) $\frac{28}{35}$

35. Which of the following numbers has a 4 in hundreths place?

(a) 423.27 (b) 0.5749

(c) 713.407 (d) 67.348

36. Which of the following is the nearest whole number of 3.748?

(a) 3 (b) 4

(c) 5 (d) 6

37. Express $\frac{4}{25}$ as a decimal ______.

(a) 0.16 (b) 0.016

(c) 0.126 (d) None of these

38. Which of the following is correct sequence of numbers in ascending order?

(a) 3.025, 3.601, 2.89, 4.23, 5.76

(b) 2.853, 3.012, 3.609, 4.502, 7.369

(c) 9.62, 8.573, 2.705, 6.43, 5.497

(d) 7.237, 5.039, 8.02, 6.076, 5.978

39. Which of the following is a correct sequence of numbers in descending order?

(a) 5.42, 6.03, 2.094, 3.746, 7.92

(b) 8.032, 7.967, 7.503, 5.207, 4.723

(c) 5.237, 6.02, 8.37, 9.143, 6.707

(d) 2.417, 4.037, 3.592, 4.759, 7.204

40. For the decimal number 807.506, what is the digit in tenths place?

(a) 5 (b) 0

(c) 6 (d) 7

41. Which of the following is the smallest decimal number?

(a) 0.4726 (b) 0.53

(c) 0.6 (d) 0.5027

42. Which of the following is the largest decimal number?

(a) 0.3974 (b) 0.7095

(c) 0.6978 (d) 0.802

43. For the number 576.4389, which digit has minimum value?

(a) 3 (b) 4

(c) 8 (d) 9

44. What is the place value of 7 in 43.076?

(a) 7 (b) 70

(c) $\frac{7}{10}$ (d) $\frac{7}{100}$

45. Which of the following is the largest fraction?

(a) $\frac{7}{9}$ (b) $\frac{2}{3}$

(c) $\frac{5}{8}$ (d) $\frac{7}{11}$

46. Which of the following is the smallest fraction?

(a) $\frac{11}{13}$ (b) $\frac{13}{17}$

(c) $\frac{7}{9}$ (d) $\frac{17}{19}$

47. Express $1\frac{5}{7}$ as a decimal to 3 decimal places?

(a) 1.174 (b) 1.714

(c) 1.724 (d) 1.741

48. Which of the following is an unlike fraction of $\frac{7}{13}$?

(a) $\frac{2}{13}$ (b) $\frac{1}{13}$

(c) $\frac{4}{13}$ (d) $\frac{5}{17}$

49. Which of the following fractions is equivalent to $\frac{1}{3}$?

(a) $\frac{2}{5}$ (b) $\frac{3}{9}$

(c) $\frac{4}{8}$ (d) $\frac{5}{12}$

50. Which of the following fractions is equivalent to $\frac{4}{17}$?

(a) $\frac{6}{17}$ (b) $\frac{7}{17}$

(c) $\frac{16}{68}$ (d) $\frac{16}{85}$

51. What is the sum of 7.007, 7.067 and 7.027?

(a) 21.111 (b) 21.011

(c) 21.101 (d) 21.121

52. What is the difference between 12.002 and 12.863?

(a) 0.761 (b) 0.861

(c) 0.961 (d) 0.869

53. Which of the following is the smallest fraction?

(a) $\frac{2}{7}$ (b) $\frac{3}{5}$

(c) $\frac{1}{8}$ (d) $\frac{7}{9}$

54. Which of the following is the largest fraction?

(a) $\frac{2}{13}$ (b) $\frac{3}{17}$

(c) $\frac{7}{15}$ (d) $\frac{8}{19}$

55. What is the value of 4.003 × 7.03 ?

(a) 27.841 (b) 28.141

(c) 28.241 (d) 28.341

56. Which of the following is the largest?

(a) 1.029 (b) 1.097

(c) 1.079 (d) 1.109

57. Which of the following is the smallest?

(a) 2.003 (b) 2.007

(c) 2.103 (d) 2.907

58. What is the product of 3.007 and 7.027?

(a) 21.13 (b) 20.83

(c) 21.23 (d) 21.33

59. What will be the result if 79.997 is subtracted from 100?

(a) 20.203 (b) 20.003

(c) 20.103 (d) 20.403

60. Which of the following is in ascending order?

(a) 7.07, 7.17, 7.927, 7.007

(b) 5.007, 5.072, 5.707, 5.777

(c) 9.02, 8.917, 7.907, 7.779

(d) 6.906, 6.792, 6.479, 6.446

☺☺☺

Darken Your Choice with HB Pencil

1.	ⓐ	ⓑ	ⓒ	ⓓ	13.	ⓐ	ⓑ	ⓒ	ⓓ	25.	ⓐ	ⓑ	ⓒ	ⓓ	37.	ⓐ	ⓑ	ⓒ	ⓓ	49.	ⓐ	ⓑ	ⓒ	ⓓ
2.	ⓐ	ⓑ	ⓒ	ⓓ	14.	ⓐ	ⓑ	ⓒ	ⓓ	26.	ⓐ	ⓑ	ⓒ	ⓓ	38.	ⓐ	ⓑ	ⓒ	ⓓ	50.	ⓐ	ⓑ	ⓒ	ⓓ
3.	ⓐ	ⓑ	ⓒ	ⓓ	15.	ⓐ	ⓑ	ⓒ	ⓓ	27.	ⓐ	ⓑ	ⓒ	ⓓ	39.	ⓐ	ⓑ	ⓒ	ⓓ	51.	ⓐ	ⓑ	ⓒ	ⓓ
4.	ⓐ	ⓑ	ⓒ	ⓓ	16.	ⓐ	ⓑ	ⓒ	ⓓ	28.	ⓐ	ⓑ	ⓒ	ⓓ	40.	ⓐ	ⓑ	ⓒ	ⓓ	52.	ⓐ	ⓑ	ⓒ	ⓓ
5.	ⓐ	ⓑ	ⓒ	ⓓ	17.	ⓐ	ⓑ	ⓒ	ⓓ	29.	ⓐ	ⓑ	ⓒ	ⓓ	41.	ⓐ	ⓑ	ⓒ	ⓓ	53.	ⓐ	ⓑ	ⓒ	ⓓ
6.	ⓐ	ⓑ	ⓒ	ⓓ	18.	ⓐ	ⓑ	ⓒ	ⓓ	30.	ⓐ	ⓑ	ⓒ	ⓓ	42.	ⓐ	ⓑ	ⓒ	ⓓ	54.	ⓐ	ⓑ	ⓒ	ⓓ
7.	ⓐ	ⓑ	ⓒ	ⓓ	19.	ⓐ	ⓑ	ⓒ	ⓓ	31.	ⓐ	ⓑ	ⓒ	ⓓ	43.	ⓐ	ⓑ	ⓒ	ⓓ	55.	ⓐ	ⓑ	ⓒ	ⓓ
8.	ⓐ	ⓑ	ⓒ	ⓓ	20.	ⓐ	ⓑ	ⓒ	ⓓ	32.	ⓐ	ⓑ	ⓒ	ⓓ	44.	ⓐ	ⓑ	ⓒ	ⓓ	56.	ⓐ	ⓑ	ⓒ	ⓓ
9.	ⓐ	ⓑ	ⓒ	ⓓ	21.	ⓐ	ⓑ	ⓒ	ⓓ	33.	ⓐ	ⓑ	ⓒ	ⓓ	45.	ⓐ	ⓑ	ⓒ	ⓓ	57.	ⓐ	ⓑ	ⓒ	ⓓ
10.	ⓐ	ⓑ	ⓒ	ⓓ	22.	ⓐ	ⓑ	ⓒ	ⓓ	34.	ⓐ	ⓑ	ⓒ	ⓓ	46.	ⓐ	ⓑ	ⓒ	ⓓ	58.	ⓐ	ⓑ	ⓒ	ⓓ
11.	ⓐ	ⓑ	ⓒ	ⓓ	23.	ⓐ	ⓑ	ⓒ	ⓓ	35.	ⓐ	ⓑ	ⓒ	ⓓ	47.	ⓐ	ⓑ	ⓒ	ⓓ	59.	ⓐ	ⓑ	ⓒ	ⓓ
12.	ⓐ	ⓑ	ⓒ	ⓓ	24.	ⓐ	ⓑ	ⓒ	ⓓ	36.	ⓐ	ⓑ	ⓒ	ⓓ	48.	ⓐ	ⓑ	ⓒ	ⓓ	60.	ⓐ	ⓑ	ⓒ	ⓓ

WORKBOOK

4 Least Common Multiple and Highest Common Factor

- A number is said to be a factor if the number has multiple part of some other numbers.

$$3 \times 2 = 6$$

Hence, 2 and 3 are factors of 6.

- A number can have many factors.

Example : Find all the factors of 20

$$20 = 1 \times 20$$

$$20 = 2 \times 10$$

$$20 = 2 \times 2 \times 5$$

So, 1, 2, 4, 5, 10 and 20 are factors of 20

- **Common Factors :** If some factors are same for two or more numbers, then the factors that are common are called common factors of those numbers.

Example : Find common factors of 15, 30 and 105.

Factors of 15 = 1, 3, 5, 15

Factors of 30 = 1, 2, 3, 5, 6, 10, 15, 30

Factors of 105 = 1, 3, 5, 7, 15, 21, 35, 105

The common factors of 15, 30 and 105 are 1, 3, 5, 15

- **Highest Common Factor (H.C.F.) :** The largest common factor of two or more numbers is called highest common factor of the given numbers.
- Multiple is formed by multiplying a given number by the counting numbers.

Example : Multiples of 3 are 3, 6, 9, 12......

- **Least Common Multiple (LCM) :** The smallest number that is a multiple of two or more numbers is called L.C.M.

Example : Least common multiple of 4 and 5

Multiples of 4 = 4, 8, 12, 16, 20, 24,......

Multiples of 5 = 5, 10, 15, 20, 25, 30,......

Least common multiple of 4 and 5 = 20

- L.C.M. × H.C.F. = Product of two numbers.

Multiple Choice Questions

1. The LCM of three different numbers is 120. Which of the given numbers cannot be their HCF?
   (a) 35 (b) 24
   (c) 12 (d) 8
2. The least number which when divided by 12, 15, 20 and 54 leaves the remainder 6 is _____.
   (a) 526 (b) 536
   (c) 546 (d) 556
3. Which of the following is the greatest number that will divide 43,91 and 183 so as to leave the same remainder in each case?
   (a) 4 (b) 6
   (c) 7 (d) 9
4. Which of the following is the least common multiple of 7, 15, 18 and 27?
   (a) 1872 (b) 1880
   (c) 1890 (d) 1896
5. The largest number which can divide 1356, 1868 and 2764 leaving the same remainder 12 in each case is _____.
   (a) 64 (b) 68
   (c) 72 (d) 84
6. Which of the following is the maximum number of students among whom 910 pens and 1001 notebooks can be distributed, so that each student gets equal number of pens and notebooks?
   (a) 81 (b) 87
   (c) 91 (d) 93
7. The H.C.F. of two numbers is 8, which one of the following cannot be their LCM?
   (a) 48 (b) 56
   (c) 60 (d) 24
8. Which of the following is H.C.F. of 62, 74 and 222 ?
   (a) 1 (b) 2
   (c) 3 (d) 4
9. The LCM of two numbers is 60. Which of the following cannot be their HCF?
   (a) 6 (b) 5
   (c) 8 (d) 10
10. The least number which should be added to 2487 so that the sum is exactly divisible by 3, 4, 5 and 6 is _____.
    (a) 23 (b) 33
    (c) 43 (d) 53
11. What is the greatest common factor of 392 and 462?
    (a) 12 (b) 14
    (c) 16 (d) 18
12. The product of two numbers is 4107 and their LCM is 111. Which of the following is their H.C.F.?
    (a) 37 (b) 47
    (c) 27 (d) 17
13. The H.C.F. of two numbers is 4 and their product is 6528. If one number is 96, then what is the other number?
    (a) 56 (b) 64
    (c) 68 (d) 78
14. Which of the following is the least common multiple of 6, 18, 27 and 39?
    (a) 702 (b) 704
    (c) 706 (d) 712
15. Which of the following is the greatest common divisor of 102, 153 and 289?
    (a) 13 (b) 17
    (c) 19 (d) 23

16. Which of the following is the greatest common divisor of 171, 361 and 513?

(a) 13 (b) 17

(c) 19 (d) 29

17. Which of the following is H.C.F. of 204, 1190 and 1445?

(a) 13 (b) 17

(c) 19 (d) 21

18. What is the L.C.M. of 22, 54, 108, 135 and 198?

(a) 1340 (b) 1980

(c) 5940 (d) 5960

19. The largest number that exactly divides 105, 1001 and 2436 is _____.

(a) 3 (b) 7

(c) 9 (d) 11

20. Six bells commence tolling together and toll at 2, 4, 6, 8, 10 and 12 seconds respectively. In one hour, how many times do they toll together?

(a) 29 (b) 30

(c) 31 (d) 32

21. The greatest number which on dividing 1657 and 2037 leaves remainder 6 and 5 respectively is _____.

(a) 117 (b) 127

(c) 137 (d) 147

22. The least number which when divided by 12, 15, 20 and 54 leaves in each case a remainder of 3 is _____.

(a) 543 (b) 538

(c) 541 (d) 539

23. The largest number of four digits which when divided by 6, 9, 12, 15 or 18 leaves remainder as 1 is _____.

(a) 9801 (b) 8901

(c) 9901 (d) 9910

24. The greatest number which on dividing 729 and 901 leaves remainder 9 and 5 respectively is _____.

(a) 16 (b) 17

(c) 18 (d) 19

25. The L.C.M. of two numbers is 864 and H.C.F. is 144. If one number is 288, then the other is _____.

(a) 424 (b) 428

(c) 432 (d) 442

26. What is the L.C.M. of 66,75 and 130 ?

(a) 20450 (b) 21450

(c) 22450 (d) None of these

27. What is the L.C.M. of 9, 15, 27 and 30?

(a) 230 (b) 240

(c) 270 (d) 290

28. If two numbers are 60 and 75 whose L.C.M. is 300, which of the following is their H.C.F.?

(a) 12 (b) 20

(c) 15 (d) 18

29. Which of the following is the smallest perfect square which is exactly divisibly by 4, 5, 6, 15 and 18?

(a) 400 (b) 900

(c) 1600 (d) 2500

30. The smallest number which when divided by 8, 9, 12 and 15 leaves the remainder 1?

(a) 361 (b) 181

(c) 341 (d) 381

31. The smallest number which when divided by 12, 15, 21, 36, 48 leaves the remainder 7 in each case?

(a) 5027 (b) 5037

(c) 5047 (d) None of these

32. If 77 and 99 are two numbers and 11 is their H.C.F., what is their LCM?
(a) 691 (b) 693
(c) 695 (d) 967

33. What is the least common multiple of 4, 6, 7, and 9?
(a) 252 (b) 254
(c) 256 (d) 272

34. The least common multiple of 7, which leaves a remainder 4 when divided by 6, 9, 15 and 18 is ______.
(a) 354 (b) 364
(c) 374 (d) 384

35. The product of two numbers is 4107. If their H.C.F. is 37, then what is the sum of these numbers?
(a) 138 (b) 147
(c) 148 (d) 158

36. What is the least common multiple of 8, 9, 12, 16, 21?
(a) 1004 (b) 1006
(c) 1008 (d) 1018

37. What is the least common multiple of 16, 24, 30, 45 and 50?
(a) 3200 (b) 3400
(c) 3600 (d) 3800

38. Which of the following is the greatest number of four digits which is divisible by 15, 25, 40 and 75?
(a) 9200 (b) 9400
(c) 9600 (d) 9800

39. The greatest possible length which can be used to measure exactly the lengths 3 m 85 cm, 7 m and 12 m 95 cm is ______.
(a) 25 cm (b) 35 cm
(c) 45 cm (d) 65 cm

40. Which of the following is the greatest number which when divided by 1054, 2061, 2274 leaves the remainder of 4, 3 and 6 respectively?
(a) 32 (b) 36
(c) 42 (d) 48

41. The lengths of three measuring rods are 64 cm, 80 cm and 96 cm. What is the minimum length of cloth which can be measured by any of these rods?
(a) 840 cm (b) 920 cm
(c) 960 cm (d) 980 cm

42. The product of two numbers is 4107. If their H.C.F is 37, what is the difference between these two numbers?
(a) 74 (b) 72
(c) 68 (d) 64

43. What is the smallest number which when divided by 4, 6, 8, 12 and 16 leaves 2 as remainder in each case?
(a) 50 (b) 52
(c) 56 (d) 58

44. H.C.F. of two numbers is 12 and their L.C.M. is 396. If one number is 36, what is the other number?
(a) 66 (b) 76
(c) 132 (d) 156

45. H.C.F. and L.C.M. of two numbers are 44 and 264 respectively. When first number is divided by 2, then quotient is 44. What is the second number?
(a) 128 (b) 132
(c) 134 (d) 142

46. If H.C.F. of 25 and 45 is 5, then what is their L.C.M.?
(a) 125 (b) 175
(c) 225 (d) 245

47. Three numbers are in the ratio 1 : 2 : 3. If their H.C.F. is 12, then which is the largest number among them?
    (a) 24 (b) 30
    (c) 36 (d) None of these

48. Which of the following is the H.C.F. of 108, 288 and 360?
    (a) 12 (b) 18
    (c) 30 (d) 36

49. The smallest number which when diminished by 7 is divisible by 12, 16, 18, 21 and 28?
    (a) 1008 (b) 1015
    (c) 1018 (d) 1024

50. The ratio of two numbers is 3 : 4. If their H.C.F. is 4, then what is their L.C.M.?
    (a) 36 (b) 42
    (c) 48 (d) 56

Darken Your Choice with HB Pencil

1.	ⓐ ⓑ ⓒ ⓓ	11.	ⓐ ⓑ ⓒ ⓓ	21.	ⓐ ⓑ ⓒ ⓓ	31.	ⓐ ⓑ ⓒ ⓓ	41.	ⓐ ⓑ ⓒ ⓓ
2.	ⓐ ⓑ ⓒ ⓓ	12.	ⓐ ⓑ ⓒ ⓓ	22.	ⓐ ⓑ ⓒ ⓓ	32.	ⓐ ⓑ ⓒ ⓓ	42.	ⓐ ⓑ ⓒ ⓓ
3.	ⓐ ⓑ ⓒ ⓓ	13.	ⓐ ⓑ ⓒ ⓓ	23.	ⓐ ⓑ ⓒ ⓓ	33.	ⓐ ⓑ ⓒ ⓓ	43.	ⓐ ⓑ ⓒ ⓓ
4.	ⓐ ⓑ ⓒ ⓓ	14.	ⓐ ⓑ ⓒ ⓓ	24.	ⓐ ⓑ ⓒ ⓓ	34.	ⓐ ⓑ ⓒ ⓓ	44.	ⓐ ⓑ ⓒ ⓓ
5.	ⓐ ⓑ ⓒ ⓓ	15.	ⓐ ⓑ ⓒ ⓓ	25.	ⓐ ⓑ ⓒ ⓓ	35.	ⓐ ⓑ ⓒ ⓓ	45.	ⓐ ⓑ ⓒ ⓓ
6.	ⓐ ⓑ ⓒ ⓓ	16.	ⓐ ⓑ ⓒ ⓓ	26.	ⓐ ⓑ ⓒ ⓓ	36.	ⓐ ⓑ ⓒ ⓓ	46.	ⓐ ⓑ ⓒ ⓓ
7.	ⓐ ⓑ ⓒ ⓓ	17.	ⓐ ⓑ ⓒ ⓓ	27.	ⓐ ⓑ ⓒ ⓓ	37.	ⓐ ⓑ ⓒ ⓓ	47.	ⓐ ⓑ ⓒ ⓓ
8.	ⓐ ⓑ ⓒ ⓓ	18.	ⓐ ⓑ ⓒ ⓓ	28.	ⓐ ⓑ ⓒ ⓓ	38.	ⓐ ⓑ ⓒ ⓓ	48.	ⓐ ⓑ ⓒ ⓓ
9.	ⓐ ⓑ ⓒ ⓓ	19.	ⓐ ⓑ ⓒ ⓓ	29.	ⓐ ⓑ ⓒ ⓓ	39.	ⓐ ⓑ ⓒ ⓓ	49.	ⓐ ⓑ ⓒ ⓓ
10.	ⓐ ⓑ ⓒ ⓓ	20.	ⓐ ⓑ ⓒ ⓓ	30.	ⓐ ⓑ ⓒ ⓓ	40.	ⓐ ⓑ ⓒ ⓓ	50.	ⓐ ⓑ ⓒ ⓓ

WORKBOOK

5 Measurement and Temperature

- The standard unit of measuring length is metre.

  1 kilometre = 1000 metres

  1 hecto metre = 100 metres

  1 deca metre = 10 metres

  1 metre = 100 centimetres

  1 millimeter $= \frac{1}{1000}$ metres

  1 cm = 10 mm
- The standard unit for measuring mass and weight is kilogram.

  1 kilogram = 1000 grams
- Metric tons are used to measure things that are very heavy.

  1 tonne = 1000 kilograms
- **Feet and Inches**

  1 feet = 12 inches
- If the number of inches is greater than 12, divide the inches by 12, the quotient is the number of feet and the remainder is the number of extra inches.

  Example : Add 5 feet 8 inches and 3 feet 10 inches

  8 inches + 10 inches = 18 inches

  = 1 feet 6 inches
- Volume or capacity of container is the maximum amount of liquid which it can hold. The standard unit for measuring capacity is litre.

  1 kilolitre = 1000 litres

  1 decilitre = 10 litre.

  1 litre = 1000 millilitre
- **Temperature :** There are two different units or scales for measuring temperature namely Fahrenheit scale and Celsius scale.
- **Conversion from Celsius temperature to Fahrenheit :**
- Multiply the Celsius temperature by $\frac{9}{5}$
- Add 32° to adjust for the offset in the Fahrenheit scale.

Example : Convert 37°C to Fahrenheit.

$$37 \times \frac{9}{5} = \frac{333}{5} = 66.6$$

$$66.6 + 32 = 98.6°F$$

- **Fahrenheit to Celsius Conversion**

Subtract 32° to adjust for the offset in the Fahrenheit scale.

Multiply the result by $\frac{5}{9}$.

Example : Convert 98.6° F to Celsius

$$98.6 - 32 = 66.6$$

$$66.6 \times \frac{5}{9} = \frac{333}{9} = 37°C$$

- **Time :** The time between one midnight and the next midnight is called one day.

1 day = 24 hours

1 hour = 60 minutes

1 minute = 60 seconds

- A week has seven days namely Sunday, Monday, Tuesday, Wednesday, Thursday, Friday and Saturday.

A year has 12 months called calendar months.

Month	Day
January	31
February	28 or 29
March	31
April	30
May	31
June	30
July	31
August	31
September	30
October	31
November	30
December	31

Note : If name of the month is not mentioned, then one month = 30 days

There are 365 days in a year.

In leap year, there are 366 days.

1 year = 12 months.

1 week = 7 days

Multiple Choice Questions

1. To convert hours into seconds, we multiply the number of hours by ________.
   (a) 60 (b) 300
   (c) 1200 (d) 3600
2. The number of seconds in 50 minutes is ________.
   (a) 3000 sec (b) 300 sec
   (c) 360 sec (d) None of these

Directions (3–8) : Find the difference.

3. 4 feet 7 inches and 3 feet 11 inches
   (a) 6 inches (b) 8 inches
   (c) 7 inches (d) 9 inches
4. 8 km 300 m and 6 km 800 m
   (a) 1 km 300 m (b) 1 km 500 m
   (c) 1 km 200 m (d) None of these
5. 9 m 15 cm and 7 m 85 cm
   (a) 1 m 40 cm (b) 1 m 30 cm
   (c) 1 m 50 cm (d) None of these
6. 15 kg 250 gm and 12 kg 850 gm
   (a) 2 kg 250 gm (b) 2 kg 900 gm
   (c) 2 kg 200 gm (d) 2 kg 400 gm
7. 17 km 200 m and 14 km 900 m
   (a) 3 km 200 m (b) 2 km 300 m
   (c) 1 km 900 m (d) 2 km 200 m
8. 8 feet 2 inches and 6 feet 8 inches
   (a) 2 feet 8 inches (b) 2 feet 10 inches
   (c) 1 feet 6 inches (d) 1 feet 8 inches
9. How many centimeters are there in 7 metres and 40 centimetres?
   (a) 740 (b) 840
   (c) 820 (d) None of these
10. How many kilometers are there in 8000 m?
    (a) 8 (b) 9
    (c) 10 (d) None of these
11. How many tonnes are there in 140000 kg of sugar?
    (a) 14 (b) 40
    (c) 140 (d) None of these
12. How many litres are there in 2860 ml?
    (a) 2 l (b) 31
    (c) 2.86 l (d) None of these
13. How many kilograms are there in 73450 gm?
    (a) 73.450 (b) 7.345
    (c) 734.50 (d) None of these
14. How many metres are there in 2 kilometers and 300 metres?
    (a) 2300 (b) 3200
    (c) 2400 (d) 2200
15. How many grams are there in 2.3 kg?
    (a) 2030 (b) 2300
    (c) 2003 (d) None of these
16. How many metres are there in 3.7 km?
    (a) 37000 (b) 3700
    (c) 370 (d) None of these
17. How many millilitres are there in 1.7 litres?
    (a) 1700 (b) 17000
    (c) 170 (d) None of these
18. How many feet are there in 76 inches?
    (a) 6.33 (b) 6
    (c) 7 (d) None of these
19. Mohan bought a-50 litres container of oil. He used 43 litres 200 ml of it. How much oil is left in the container?
    (a) 6 litres 600 ml (b) 6 litres 800 ml
    (c) 7 litres 800 ml (d) 7 litres 200 ml
20. A jar can hold 4 litres 250 ml honey. How much honey will be needed to fill 7 such jars?
    (a) 28 litres 250 ml
    (b) 29 litres 250 ml
    (c) 28 litres 750 ml
    (d) 29 litres 750 ml

21. Ravi needs 6 containers which can hold 15 litres 600 ml oil. What is the capacity of each container?
(a) 2 litres 900 ml (b) 2 litres 400 ml
(c) 2 litres 800 ml (d) 2 litres 600 ml

Directions (22–25) : Add the following.

22. 27 litres 850 ml and 19 litres 375 ml
(a) 47 litres 275 ml
(b) 47 litres 225 ml
(c) 47 litres 325 ml
(d) 46 litres 625 ml

23. 56 litres 285 ml and 64 litres 885 ml
(a) 121 litres 180 ml
(b) 121 litres 170 ml
(c) 121 litres 190 ml
(d) 121 litres 210 ml

24. 16 litres 450 ml and 17 litres and 695 ml
(a) 34 litres 45 ml (b) 34 litres 245 ml
(c) 33 litres 845 ml (d) 34 litres 145 ml

25. 39 l 650 ml and 43 l 550 ml
(a) 83 l 300 ml (b) 83 l 200 ml
(c) 83 l 400 ml (d) None of these

26. How many minutes are there in 7 hours 20 minutes?
(a) 420 (b) 440
(c) 430 (d) 450

27. How many days are there in 7 months?
(a) 212 (b) 210
(c) 211 (d) 213

28. How many days are there in 15 weeks and 2 days?
(a) 107 (b) 115
(c) 122 (d) None of these

29. How many weeks are there in 364 days?
(a) 51 (b) 52
(c) 53 (d) None of these

30. The number of seconds in 12 minutes is ________.
(a) 840 (b) 960
(c) 720 (d) 360

31. The number of hours in 25 days is ________.
(a) 580 (b) 540
(c) 560 (d) 600

32. The number of minutes in one day is ________.
(a) 1420 (b) 1430
(c) 1440 (d) 1460

33. The number of weeks in a leap year is ________.
(a) 52 (b) 53
(c) 51 (d) 54

34. The number of days in February 1984 is ________.
(a) 28 (b) 29
(c) 27 (d) 30

35. The number of centimetre in 2 kilometres is
(a) 2000 cm (b) 20000 cm
(c) 2000000 cm (d) 200000 cm

36. The number of inches in 12 feet is ________.
(a) 154 (b) 124
(c) 134 (d) 144

37. Convert 41°F to Celcius degree.
(a) 5°C (b) 15°C
(c) 2.5°C (d) None of these

38. Convert 20°C to Fahrenheit.
(a) 58°F (b) 68°F
(c) 78°F (d) 48°F

39. Convert 25°C to Fahrenheit.
(a) 57°F (b) 67°F
(c) 77°F (d) 87°F

40. Convert 18° Fahrenheit to Celcius.
(a) 6.7°C (b) 7.7°C
(c) – 6.7°C (d) –7.7°C

41. The highest temperature ever recorded in UK was 101.3°F recorded in Kent in 2003. How many degree Celsius was this?
(a) 38.5°C (b) 56.3°C
(c) 39.5°C (d) 43.5°C

42. 100°C = ? Fahrenheit ________.
(a) 212°F (b) 214°F
(c) 216°F (d) 192°F

43. Convert 57°C to Fahrenheit.
(a) 133.6°F (b) 134°F
(c) 124.6°F (d) 134.6°F

44. Convert 90°F to Celsius.
(a) 32.2°C (b) 31.2°C
(c) 33.2°C (d) 29.2°C

45. Convert 106°F to Celsius.
(a) 39.1°C (b) 40.1°C
(c) 41.1°C (d) 43.1°C

46. Convert 40°C to Fahrenheit.
(a) 104°F (b) 102°F
(c) 105°F (d) 106°F

47. Convert 24°C to Fahrenheit.
(a) 75.2° F (b) 73.2° F
(c) 74.2° F (d) 77.2° F

48. 64° F is equal to how many ° Celsius?
(a) 17.78° C (b) 18.7° C
(c) 19.7° C (d) None of these

49. 98.6°F is equal to how many degree Celsius?
(a) 31°C (b) 36°C
(c) 37°C (d) 39°C

50. – 40°C is equal to how many Fahrenheit?
(a) 40°F (b) – 30°F
(c) – 40°F (d) None of these

☺☺☺

Darken Your Choice with HB Pencil

1.	ⓐ	ⓑ	ⓒ	ⓓ	11.	ⓐ	ⓑ	ⓒ	ⓓ	21.	ⓐ	ⓑ	ⓒ	ⓓ	31.	ⓐ	ⓑ	ⓒ	ⓓ	41.	ⓐ	ⓑ	ⓒ	ⓓ
2.	ⓐ	ⓑ	ⓒ	ⓓ	12.	ⓐ	ⓑ	ⓒ	ⓓ	22.	ⓐ	ⓑ	ⓒ	ⓓ	32.	ⓐ	ⓑ	ⓒ	ⓓ	42.	ⓐ	ⓑ	ⓒ	ⓓ
3.	ⓐ	ⓑ	ⓒ	ⓓ	13.	ⓐ	ⓑ	ⓒ	ⓓ	23.	ⓐ	ⓑ	ⓒ	ⓓ	33.	ⓐ	ⓑ	ⓒ	ⓓ	43.	ⓐ	ⓑ	ⓒ	ⓓ
4.	ⓐ	ⓑ	ⓒ	ⓓ	14.	ⓐ	ⓑ	ⓒ	ⓓ	24.	ⓐ	ⓑ	ⓒ	ⓓ	34.	ⓐ	ⓑ	ⓒ	ⓓ	44.	ⓐ	ⓑ	ⓒ	ⓓ
5.	ⓐ	ⓑ	ⓒ	ⓓ	15.	ⓐ	ⓑ	ⓒ	ⓓ	25.	ⓐ	ⓑ	ⓒ	ⓓ	35.	ⓐ	ⓑ	ⓒ	ⓓ	45.	ⓐ	ⓑ	ⓒ	ⓓ
6.	ⓐ	ⓑ	ⓒ	ⓓ	16.	ⓐ	ⓑ	ⓒ	ⓓ	26.	ⓐ	ⓑ	ⓒ	ⓓ	36.	ⓐ	ⓑ	ⓒ	ⓓ	46.	ⓐ	ⓑ	ⓒ	ⓓ
7.	ⓐ	ⓑ	ⓒ	ⓓ	17.	ⓐ	ⓑ	ⓒ	ⓓ	27.	ⓐ	ⓑ	ⓒ	ⓓ	37.	ⓐ	ⓑ	ⓒ	ⓓ	47.	ⓐ	ⓑ	ⓒ	ⓓ
8.	ⓐ	ⓑ	ⓒ	ⓓ	18.	ⓐ	ⓑ	ⓒ	ⓓ	28.	ⓐ	ⓑ	ⓒ	ⓓ	38.	ⓐ	ⓑ	ⓒ	ⓓ	48.	ⓐ	ⓑ	ⓒ	ⓓ
9.	ⓐ	ⓑ	ⓒ	ⓓ	19.	ⓐ	ⓑ	ⓒ	ⓓ	29.	ⓐ	ⓑ	ⓒ	ⓓ	39.	ⓐ	ⓑ	ⓒ	ⓓ	49.	ⓐ	ⓑ	ⓒ	ⓓ
10.	ⓐ	ⓑ	ⓒ	ⓓ	20.	ⓐ	ⓑ	ⓒ	ⓓ	30.	ⓐ	ⓑ	ⓒ	ⓓ	40.	ⓐ	ⓑ	ⓒ	ⓓ	50.	ⓐ	ⓑ	ⓒ	ⓓ

WORKBOOK

6 Money

- Money is any object or record that is generally accepted as payment for goods and services. Unit of currency in India is Rupees.

  One Rupee = 100 Paisa

- 10 coins of 10 paisa make one rupee.
- 2 coins of 50 paisa make one rupee.
- 4 coins of 25 paisa make one rupee.
- One coin of 50 paisa and 2 coins of 25 paise make one rupee.
- The paper based notes available in India are ₹ 2000 , ₹ 500, ₹ 100, ₹ 50, ₹ 20, ₹ 10 and ₹ 5.

Multiple Choice Questions

1. Mohan has ₹ 5000 in his purse. He bought a shirt of ₹ 575 and a Jeans of ₹ 1340. He also bought a pair of shoes for ₹ 1739. How much money is left with him?
   (a) ₹ 1276 (b) ₹ 1346
   (c) ₹ 1356 (d) ₹ 1286
2. Rakesh went to purchase a book and gave the cashier two coins of ₹ 10, four notes of ₹ 20, two notes of ₹ 100 and one note of ₹ 500. If the price of book is ₹ 785, then how much money did he get back?
   (a) ₹ 5 (b) ₹ 10
   (c) ₹ 15 (d) ₹ 25
3. I went to market and bought clothes for ₹ 3600, food items for ₹ 2400 and spent ₹ 125 as conveyance. What is my total expenditure?
   (a) ₹ 6225 (b) ₹ 5925
   (c) ₹ 6025 (d) ₹ 6125
4. Mohit has a note of ₹ 2000. He bought a book of ₹ 580, 8 copies of ₹ 45 each and 6 pens of ₹ 16 each. How much money is left with him?
   (a) ₹ 964 (b) ₹ 864
   (c) ₹ 1064 (d) ₹ 984
5. If the cost of one litre petrol is ₹ 71.75, then what is the cost of 4 litres petrol?
   (a) ₹ 257 (b) ₹ 267
   (c) ₹ 287 (d) ₹ 297
6. Mohan travelled in a train, the fare for up and down journey is ₹ 1440. He spends ₹ 380 on eatable and ₹ 220 on other expenses. What is the total expenses during journey?
   (a) ₹ 1840 (b) ₹ 1940
   (c) ₹ 2140 (d) ₹ 2040
7. Ankush bought two dozen of eggs at ₹ 20/ dozen. He gave a 100 rupee note to the shopkeeper. How much will Ankush get back?
   (a) ₹ 40 (b) ₹ 60
   (c) ₹ 30 (d) ₹ 50
8. Hardik gave ₹ 530 to Shyam. Shyam returned it to Hardik giving him a 2000 rupee note. How much will Hardik return to Shyam?
   (a) ₹ 1570 (b) ₹ 1470
   (c) ₹ 1370 (d) ₹ 770
9. The price of 20 apples is ₹ 50, and the price of 1 kg apples is ₹ 30. If 12 apples weigh 1 kg, then which of the following would cost the cheapest?
   (a) 25 apples (b) 2 kg apples
   (c) 3 kg apples (d) 12 apples
10. If 500 g of oranges cost ₹ 23, what is the cost of 1 kg oranges?
    (a) ₹ 60 (b) ₹ 66
    (c) ₹ 56 (d) ₹ 46
11. What is the cost of , if________.

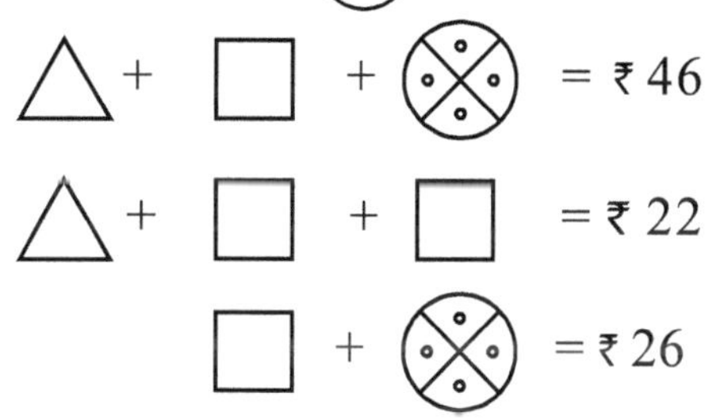

    (a) ₹ 20 (b) ₹ 22
    (c) ₹ 25 (d) ₹ 28
12. Ram has three ₹ 500 notes, four ₹ 100 notes and three ₹ 50 notes. What is the total amount that Ram has?
    (a) ₹ 2250 (b) ₹ 1950
    (c) ₹ 2150 (d) ₹ 2050
13. Mohan earns ₹ 14,600. He spent ₹ 2400 on house rent, 1500 on clothes, 2600 on food and 2300 on education. What is the saving of Mohan?
    (a) ₹ 7800 (b) ₹ 5600
    (c) ₹ 5800 (d) ₹ 6800

14. I bought 25 sweets, each costing ₹ 12. I paid ₹ 500 to the shopkeeper. What amount will be returned?
(a) ₹ 200 (b) ₹ 300
(c) ₹ 250 (d) ₹ 350

15. Rashmi has two ₹ 2000 notes, one ₹ 500 note and one ₹ 100 note. What is the total amount Rashmi has?
(a) ₹ 4300 (b) ₹ 4600
(c) ₹ 5600 (d) ₹ 4800

16. In a hotel, Ramesh has 2 plates of vegetables each costing ₹ 130, 6 nans, each costing ₹ 18 and 2 ice creams each costing ₹ 56. What is the total bill Ramesh has to pay?
(a) ₹ 560 (b) ₹ 460
(c) ₹ 480 (d) ₹ 580

17. Gouri has two ₹ 500 notes, seven ₹ 100 notes, six ₹ 50 notes and five ₹ 20 notes. What is the total amount Gouri has?
(a) ₹ 1900 (b) ₹ 2100
(c) ₹ 2300 (d) ₹ 2000

18. If 10 days of working pays ₹ 230, then how much can a person earn by working 30 days in a month?
(a) ₹ 570 (b) ₹ 690
(c) ₹ 790 (d) ₹ 1030

19. The cost of ice cream is ₹ 8, how many coins can be taken to buy it?
(a) one 2 rupee coin, one 1 rupee coin, and, one 5-rupee coin.
(b) One 2 rupee coin, one 1 rupee coin, and no 5-rupee coins.
(c) Two 2 rupee coins, and three 1 rupee coins.
(d) None of these

20. Sunny has five two rupee coins and two notes of 50 rupees each. Which of the following items can he buy?
(a) A toy worth ₹ 160
(b) One kg cashew worth ₹ 470
(c) One kg ice-cream worth ₹ 170
(d) One kg tomato worth ₹ 110

21. The cost of fencing a square field of side 5 m is ₹ 300. What will be the cost of fencing per metre?
(a) ₹ 10 (b) ₹ 15
(c) ₹ 20 (d) ₹ 22

22. The perimeter of a square field is 24 m, and the cost of ploughing is ₹ 300/m^2. How much will it cost to plough the field?
(a) ₹ 9700 (b) ₹ 10700
(c) ₹ 10,800 (d) ₹ 19,700

Directions (23-27) : Study the given table, and answer the following questions.

	Item	**Cost (per pc.)**
P		₹ 770
Q		₹ 310
R		₹ 170
S		₹ 320

23. What is the cost of items S and P together?
(a) ₹ 1080 (b) ₹ 990
(c) ₹ 1090 (d) ₹ 1190

24. What is the difference in the cost of the costliest item and the cheapest item?
(a) ₹ 670 (b) ₹ 600
(c) ₹ 560 (d) ₹ 150

25. What is the combined cost of all the items?

(a) ₹ 1670 (b) ₹ 1560

(c) ₹ 1660 (d) ₹ 1570

26. Ram has ₹ 1360 with him. Which of the following sets can he buy?
    (a) P, Q and R (b) P, R, Q and S
    (c) P, Q and s (d) All of these

27. What is the cost of two P and three Q, put together?
    (a) ₹ 2060 (b) ₹ 2470
    (c) ₹ 1620 (d) ₹ 2260

28. Mohit has a note of ₹ 2000. He bought a school bag for ₹ 760, a book of Maths for ₹ 340 and 15 notebooks, each notebook costing ₹40. How much money is left with him?
    (a) ₹ 300 (b) ₹ 350
    (c) ₹ 400 (d) ₹ 450

29. The price of apples is ₹ 250 per kg. How much apples can Mr. Sharma buy for ₹ 1000?
    (a) 3 kg (b) 4 kg
    (c) 5 kg (d) 8 kg

30. The cost of a pair of jeans is ₹ 875, the cost of a cotton T-Shirt is ₹ 435 and the cost of a towel is ₹ 175. What is the total cost of these articles?
    (a) ₹ 1465 b) ₹ 1475
    (c) ₹ 1485 (d) ₹ 1495

Darken Your Choice with HB Pencil

1.	ⓐ	ⓑ	ⓒ	ⓓ	7.	ⓐ	ⓑ	ⓒ	ⓓ	13.	ⓐ	ⓑ	ⓒ	ⓓ	19.	ⓐ	ⓑ	ⓒ	ⓓ	25.	ⓐ	ⓑ	ⓒ	ⓓ
2.	ⓐ	ⓑ	ⓒ	ⓓ	8.	ⓐ	ⓑ	ⓒ	ⓓ	14.	ⓐ	ⓑ	ⓒ	ⓓ	20.	ⓐ	ⓑ	ⓒ	ⓓ	26.	ⓐ	ⓑ	ⓒ	ⓓ
3.	ⓐ	ⓑ	ⓒ	ⓓ	9.	ⓐ	ⓑ	ⓒ	ⓓ	15.	ⓐ	ⓑ	ⓒ	ⓓ	21.	ⓐ	ⓑ	ⓒ	ⓓ	27.	ⓐ	ⓑ	ⓒ	ⓓ
4.	ⓐ	ⓑ	ⓒ	ⓓ	10.	ⓐ	ⓑ	ⓒ	ⓓ	16.	ⓐ	ⓑ	ⓒ	ⓓ	22.	ⓐ	ⓑ	ⓒ	ⓓ	28.	ⓐ	ⓑ	ⓒ	ⓓ
5.	ⓐ	ⓑ	ⓒ	ⓓ	11.	ⓐ	ⓑ	ⓒ	ⓓ	17.	ⓐ	ⓑ	ⓒ	ⓓ	23.	ⓐ	ⓑ	ⓒ	ⓓ	29.	ⓐ	ⓑ	ⓒ	ⓓ
6.	ⓐ	ⓑ	ⓒ	ⓓ	12.	ⓐ	ⓑ	ⓒ	ⓓ	18.	ⓐ	ⓑ	ⓒ	ⓓ	24.	ⓐ	ⓑ	ⓒ	ⓓ	30.	ⓐ	ⓑ	ⓒ	ⓓ

WORKBOOK

7 Ratio and Proportion

- Ratio is used to make comparisons between two or more things. Ratio is generally expressed in its simplest form.
- If a and b are two numbers, then their ratio is expressed as $a:b$ or $\frac{a}{b}$

  Here a is called antecedent and b is called consequent.
- Ratio has no units.
- If we multiply or divide the numerator and denominator of a ratio with the same number, the ratio remains same.
- **Comparison of Ratios :**

  We can find greater or lesser ratio in a pair of two or more ratios.

  Example : Which one of the following two ratios is greater?

  $$4 : 5 \text{ or } 5 : 6$$

  Solution : 4 : 5, 5 : 6

  $$\frac{4}{5}, \frac{5}{6}$$

  LCM of 5, 6 = 30

  $$\frac{4}{5} = \frac{24}{30} \text{ and } \frac{5}{6} = \frac{25}{30}$$

  $$\therefore \quad 5 : 6 > 4 : 5$$

  Proportion : A proportion is a statement of the equality of two ratios.

  It is denoted as $a : b :: c : d$.
- a, b, c, d are the 1st, 2nd, 3rd and 4th terms of the proportion.

  $$\frac{a}{b} = \frac{c}{d}$$

  $$a \times d = b \times c$$

  Here a and d are called extremes and b and c are called means.
- **For a Proportion :**

  Product of extremes = Product of means

Multiple Choice Questions

1. If first, third and fourth terms of a proportion are 16, 36 and 54, then second term is ______.
   (a) 18 (b) 24
   (c) 30 (d) 32
2. The length and breadth of a rectangle are in the ratio 3 : 1. If the breadth is 8 cm, then the length of the rectangle is ______.
   (a) 16 cm (b) 24 cm
   (c) 32 cm (d) 36 cm
3. Two numbers are in the ratio 7 : 9. If the sum of the numbers is 112, then the smaller number is ______.
   (a) 42 (b) 49
   (c) 63 (d) 72
4. Two numbers are in the ratio 7 : 9. If the sum of the numbers is 144, then what is the difference between the numbers?
   (a) 63 (b) 81
   (c) 27 (d) 18
5. For what value of x the numbers 3, 18, x, 42 are in proportion?
   (a) 6 (b) 7
   (c) 8 (d) 9
6. If the ratio of ages of Lina and Mina is 6 : 5 at present and 15 years hence, this ratio will be 9 : 8, then what is the present age of Mina?
   (a) 15 years (b) 20 years
   (c) 25 years (d) 30 years
7. The present ratio of ages of Amir and Sonal is 4 : 5. 18 years ago this ratio was 11 : 16. What is the present age of Amir?
   (a) 32 years (b) 36 years
   (c) 40 years (d) 42 years
8. ₹ 1162 is divided among Anil, Ankit and Raju in the ratio 35 : 28 : 37. What is the share of Ankit?
   (a) ₹ 372.12 (b) ₹ 325.36
   (c) ₹ 392.43 (d) ₹ 412.50
9. If $\frac{x}{5} = \frac{y}{8}$ then what is the ratio between $(x + 5)$ and $(y + 8)$?
   (a) 5 : 8 (b) 8 : 5
   (c) 5 : 3 (d) 3 : 5
10. Two numbers are in the ratio 3 : 5. If 9 is subtracted from each, the new numbers are in the ratio 12 : 23. What is the smaller number?
    (a) 33 (b) 36
    (c) 48 (d) 56
11. The ratio of three numbers is 3 : 4 : 7 and their product is 18144. Which is the largest number?
    (a) 18 (b) 21
    (c) 24 (d) 42
12. A certain amount was divided between Manoj and Rajesh in the ratio 4 : 3. If Rajesh's share is ₹ 4800, what is the share of Manoj?
    (a) 5600 (b) 6400
    (c) 6800 (d) 7200
13. The average age of three students is 25 years. Their ages are in the ratio 3 : 5 : 7. What is the age of the youngest student?
    (a) 12 years (b) 15 years
    (c) 18 years (d) 21 years
14. In a school, the ratio of number of boys to girls is 8 : 5. If there are 160 girls, then what is total strength of the school?
    (a) 256 (b) 276
    (c) 396 (d) 416
15. The ratio of three numbers is 3 : 4 : 7 and their product is 10500. What is the smallest number among them?
    (a) 14 (b) 15
    (c) 18 (d) 24
16. There are 210 coins in a box of ₹ one and fifty paisa only. The ratio of their respective values is 13 : 11. What is the number of one rupee coins?
    (a) 38 (b) 58
    (c) 68 (d) 78
17. Mohit earns ₹ 16,400 and saves ₹ 9000 in a month. What is the ratio of his expenses to his saving?
    (a) 17 : 25 (b) 37 : 45
    (c) 27 : 41 (d) None of these

18. If 49, P, P, 16 are in proportion, then what is the value of P?
(a) 14 (b) 28
(c) 42 (d) 56

19. Ramesh earns ₹ 14,800 and saves ₹ 3,200 per month. What is the ratio of his saving and expenditure?
(a) 6 : 29 (b) 7 : 29
(c) 8 : 29 (d) None of these

20. If 8100 is divided among Akash, Sumit and Nandan in the ratio 2 : 3 : 4, then what is the share of Sumit?
(a) ₹ 1800 (b) ₹ 2400
(c) ₹ 2500 (d) ₹ 2700

21. ₹ 2040 is divided among Milan, Karim, and Shekhar in the ratio 2 : 3 : 5. What is the share of Shekhar?
(a) ₹ 1020 (b) ₹ 1120
(c) ₹ 920 (d) ₹ 840

22. The angles of a triangle are in the ratio 2 : 3 : 4. What is the measure of smallest angle?
(a) 40° (b) 54°
(c) 72° (d) 90°

23. What is the ratio of 30 seconds to 1 hour?
(a) 1 : 60 (b) 1 : 120
(c) 1 : 240 (d) 1 : 360

24. What is the ratio of 75 cm to 2 metres?
(a) 2 : 3 (b) 1 : 3
(c) 3 : 8 (d) 1 : 8

25. What is the ratio of 4.5 m to 30 cm?
(a) 5 : 1 (b) 15 : 1
(c) 25 : 1 (d) 45 : 1

26. What is the ratio of 6 hours to 2 days?
(a) 1 : 4 (b) 1 : 6
(c) 1 : 8 (d) 1 : 10

27. In a class there are 124 students. If number of girls is 42, then what is the ratio of girls to boys in that class?
(a) 1 : 2 (b) 1 : 3
(c) 2 : 1 (d) 21 : 41

28. In a class there are 36 girls and 108 boys. What is the ratio of boys to total number of students?
(a) 1 : 4 (b) 1 : 2
(c) 3 : 4 (d) 4 : 3

29. The ratio of 1 hour to 400 seconds is ______.
(a) 1 : 9 (b) 9 : 1
(c) 1 : 8 (d) 8 : 1

30. 7 : 17 is equivalent to ______.
(a) 14 : 68 (b) 21 : 51
(c) 49 : 85 (d) 28 : 102

31. A bag contains 50 paisa, 25 paisa and 10 paisa coins in the ratio 5 : 9 : 4 amounting to ₹ 206. What is the number of 25 paisa coins?
(a) 300 (b) 320
(c) 340 (d) 360

32. If 2A = 3B = 4C, then A : B : C is ______.
(a) 3 : 4 : 6 (b) 6 : 4 : 3
(c) 4 : 3 : 1 (d) None of these

33. Two whole numbers whose sum is 72 cannot be in the ratio ______.
(a) 5 : 7 (b) 3 : 5
(c) 3 : 4 (d) 4 : 5

34. Which of the following ratios is the smallest?
(a) 17 : 25 (b) 15 : 23
(c) 7 : 15 (d) 21 : 29

35. Which of the following ratios is the greatest?
(a) 7 : 15 (b) 8 : 17
(c) 9 : 16 (d) 11 : 25

36. If ₹ 12100 were divided among L, M, N in the ratio 45 : 36 : 40, then what is the share of N?
(a) ₹ 4000 (b) ₹ 6000
(c) ₹ 4800 (d) ₹ 6400

37. The ratio between two numbers is 3 : 4 and their LCM is 180. What is the difference between two numbers?
(a) 12 (b) 15
(c) 18 (d) 20

38. What is the fourth proportional to 4, 9, 12?
(a) 15 (b) 18
(c) 24 (d) 27

39. What is the third proportional to 16 and 36?
(a) 63 (b) 72
(c) 81 (d) 99

40. What will be the ratio between the area and perimeter of a rectangle of measure 11 cm by 8 cm?
   (a) 11 : 8 (b) 88 : 19
   (c) 44 : 19 (d) 8 : 11

41. Two numbers are in the ratio 5 : 4. If their sum is 324. What is the difference between the numbers?
   (a) 18 (b) 36
   (c) 42 (d) 44

42. A 49 cm line segment is divided into two parts in the ratio 3 : 4. What is the measure of the smaller part?
   (a) 21 cm (b) 18 cm
   (c) 24 cm (d) None of these

43. If 36 : 81 :: m : 63, what is the value of m?
   (a) 14 (b) 28
   (c) 42 (d) 56

44. What is the ratio of 40 cm to 1 km?
   (a) 1 : 20000 (b) 1 : 10000
   (c) 1 : 5000 (d) 1 : 2500

45. What is the ratio of 6 inches of 3 feet?
   (a) 1 : 3 (b) 1 : 4
   (c) 1 : 6 (d) 1 : 8

46. The cost of 5 pens is ₹ 65 and cost of 12 pencils is ₹ 84. What is the ratio of cost of a pencil to cost of a pen?
   (a) 16 : 7 (b) 15 : 7
   (c) 7 : 13 (d) 13 : 7

47. The temperature of a day in June is 37°C and the temperature of a day in September is 68°F. What is the ratio between the two?
   (a) 20 : 37 (b) 37 : 20
   (c) 10 : 37 (d) 37 : 10

48. The difference between two numbers is 10 and the ratio between them is 5 : 3. What is the sum of the numbers?
   (a) 30 (b) 35
   (c) 40 (d) 45

49. If two times of x is equal to three times of y and also equal to four times of z. What is the value of $x : y : z$?
   (a) 1 : 2 : 3 (b) 2 : 3 : 4
   (c) 4 : 3 : 2 (d) 6 : 4 : 3

50. Two numbers are in the ratio 7 : 9. If the sum of numbers is 240, then the larger number is ________.
   (a) 105 (b) 115
   (c) 125 (d) 135

Darken Your Choice with HB Pencil

1. ⓐ ⓑ ⓒ ⓓ	11. ⓐ ⓑ ⓒ ⓓ	21. ⓐ ⓑ ⓒ ⓓ	31. ⓐ ⓑ ⓒ ⓓ	41. ⓐ ⓑ ⓒ ⓓ
2. ⓐ ⓑ ⓒ ⓓ	12. ⓐ ⓑ ⓒ ⓓ	22. ⓐ ⓑ ⓒ ⓓ	32. ⓐ ⓑ ⓒ ⓓ	42. ⓐ ⓑ ⓒ ⓓ
3. ⓐ ⓑ ⓒ ⓓ	13. ⓐ ⓑ ⓒ ⓓ	23. ⓐ ⓑ ⓒ ⓓ	33. ⓐ ⓑ ⓒ ⓓ	43. ⓐ ⓑ ⓒ ⓓ
4. ⓐ ⓑ ⓒ ⓓ	14. ⓐ ⓑ ⓒ ⓓ	24. ⓐ ⓑ ⓒ ⓓ	34. ⓐ ⓑ ⓒ ⓓ	44. ⓐ ⓑ ⓒ ⓓ
5. ⓐ ⓑ ⓒ ⓓ	15. ⓐ ⓑ ⓒ ⓓ	25. ⓐ ⓑ ⓒ ⓓ	35. ⓐ ⓑ ⓒ ⓓ	45. ⓐ ⓑ ⓒ ⓓ
6. ⓐ ⓑ ⓒ ⓓ	16. ⓐ ⓑ ⓒ ⓓ	26. ⓐ ⓑ ⓒ ⓓ	36. ⓐ ⓑ ⓒ ⓓ	46. ⓐ ⓑ ⓒ ⓓ
7. ⓐ ⓑ ⓒ ⓓ	17. ⓐ ⓑ ⓒ ⓓ	27. ⓐ ⓑ ⓒ ⓓ	37. ⓐ ⓑ ⓒ ⓓ	47. ⓐ ⓑ ⓒ ⓓ
8. ⓐ ⓑ ⓒ ⓓ	18. ⓐ ⓑ ⓒ ⓓ	28. ⓐ ⓑ ⓒ ⓓ	38. ⓐ ⓑ ⓒ ⓓ	48. ⓐ ⓑ ⓒ ⓓ
9. ⓐ ⓑ ⓒ ⓓ	19. ⓐ ⓑ ⓒ ⓓ	29. ⓐ ⓑ ⓒ ⓓ	39. ⓐ ⓑ ⓒ ⓓ	49. ⓐ ⓑ ⓒ ⓓ
10. ⓐ ⓑ ⓒ ⓓ	20. ⓐ ⓑ ⓒ ⓓ	30. ⓐ ⓑ ⓒ ⓓ	40. ⓐ ⓑ ⓒ ⓓ	50. ⓐ ⓑ ⓒ ⓓ

8 WORKBOOK

Area, Perimeter and Volume

- The area of a plane figure is the measure of surface area enclosed by its boundary.

  Area of rectangle = Length × Breadth

  Diagonal of rectangle $= \sqrt{(\text{Length})^2 + (\text{Breadth})^2}$

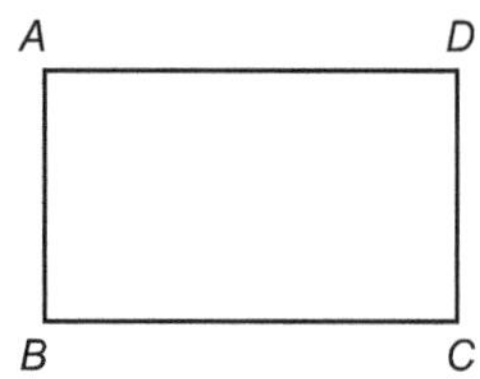

  Perimeter of rectangle = 2 (Length + Breadth)

- **Square :**

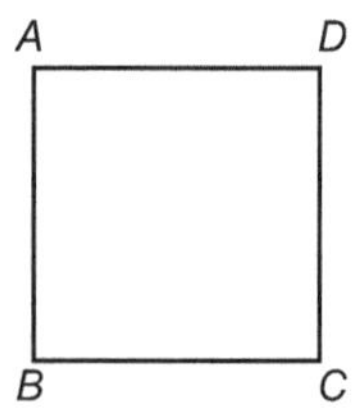

  Area of square = $(\text{side})^2$

  Perimeter of square = 4 × side

  Diagonal of square $= \sqrt{2} \times \text{side}$

- **Area of Triangle :**

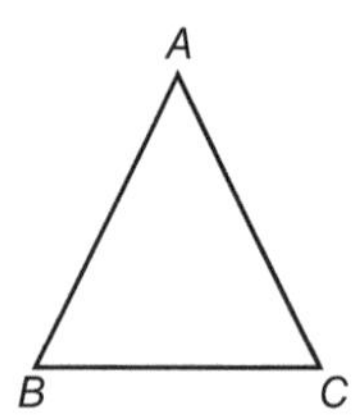

$$s = \frac{a+b+c}{2}$$

$$\text{Area} = \sqrt{s(s-a)(s-b)(s-c)}$$

Area of right angle triangle $= \frac{1}{2} \times \text{base} \times \text{height}$

Area of equilateral triangle $= \frac{\sqrt{3}}{4} \times (\text{side})^2$

Perimeter of triangle = $a + b + c$

- **Circle :** Diameter = 2 × Radius

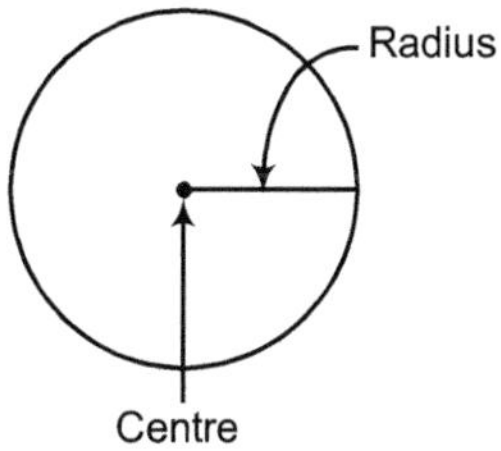

Circumference = $2\pi r = \pi d$

Area = πr^2

- **Cuboid :** Surface area of cuboid = $2(lb + bh + lh)$

Diagonal of cuboid $= \sqrt{l^2 + b^2 + h^2}$

Volume of cuboid $= lbh$

- **Cube :** Surface area of cube = $6a^2$

Diagonal of cube $= a\sqrt{3}$

Volume of cube = a^3

Multiple Choice Questions

1. The perimeter of a square is 44 cm. What is its area?
   (a) 121 cm^2 (b) 144 cm^2
   (c) 169 cm^2 (d) None of these
2. The perimeter of a rectangle is 42 cm. If its length is 15 cm what is its breadth?
   (a) 6 cm (b) 7 cm
   (c) 8 cm (d) 9 cm
3. The length and breadth of a rectangle are 15 cm and 12 cm respectively. What is its area?
   (a) 120 cm^2 (b) 140 cm^2
   (c) 160 cm^2 (d) 180 cm^2
4. The side of a square is 8 cm. What is the length of its diagonal?
   (a) $4\sqrt{2}$ cm (b) $6\sqrt{2}$ cm
   (c) $8\sqrt{2}$ cm (d) None of these
5. The length of diagonal of a square is $6\sqrt{2}$ cm. What is its area?
   (a) 25 cm^2 (b) 28 cm^2
   (c) 32 cm^2 (d) 36 cm^2
6. The length and breadth of a rectangle are 12 cm and 5 cm. What is the length of its diagonal?
   (a) 13 cm (b) 14 cm
   (c) 15 cm (d) 17 cm
7. The circumference of a circle is 176 cm. What is its area?
   (a) 2864 cm^2 (b) 2446 cm^2
   (c) 2464 cm^2 (d) 2644 cm^2
8. The diameter of a circle is 14 cm.What is its area?
   (a) 14 cm^2 (b) 154 cm^2
   (c) 164 cm^2 (d) 184 cm^2
9. The sides of a triangle are 10 cm, 24 cm, and 26 cm. What is its area?
   (a) 90 cm^2 (b) 120 cm^2
   (c) 240 cm^2 (d) None of these
10. The side of an equilateral triangle is 8 cm. What is its area?
    (a) $16\sqrt{3}$ cm^2 (b) $24\sqrt{3}$ cm^2
    (c) $32\sqrt{3}$ cm^2 (d) $64\sqrt{3}$ cm^2
11. If the length of diagonal of a square is 20 cm. What is its perimeter?
    (a) $10\sqrt{2}$ cm (b) 40 cm
    (c) $40\sqrt{2}$ cm (d) 200 cm
12. The sides of a rectangular field are in the ratio 3 : 4. If the area of the field is 7500 m^2, then what is the perimeter of this rectangular field?
    (a) 350 m (b) 250 m
    (c) 280 m (d) 380 m
13. If length of rectangle is 15 m and its diagonal is 17 m. What is the area of rectangle?
    (a) 120 m^2 (b) 112 m^2
    (c) 124 m^2 (d) 240 m^2
14. The diagonal of a square is $4\sqrt{2}$ cm. What is its perimeter?
    (a) 12 cm (b) 16 cm
    (c) 20 cm (d) 24 cm
15. The diagonal of a square is $8\sqrt{2}$ cm. What is its area?
    (a) 16 cm^2 (b) 36 cm^2
    (c) 64 cm^2 (d) None of these
16. The area of rectangle is 96 m^2. If its breadth is 8 m. What is its perimeter ?
    (a) 20 m (b) 40 m
    (c) 60 m (d) 80 m
17. The length and breadth of a rectangle are in the ratio 7 : 3. If its perimeter is 60 cm, what is its area?
    (a) 189 cm^2 (b) 198 cm^2
    (c) 169 cm^2 (d) 209 cm^2
18. Find area of the parallelogram shown in the figure.

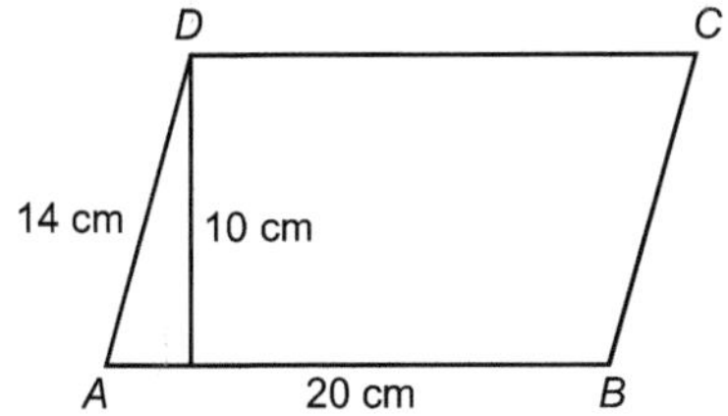

(a) 140 cm^2 (b) 180 cm^2
(c) 200 cm^2 (d) 240 cm^2

19. If the perimeter of given figure is 36 m. What is the length of DE?

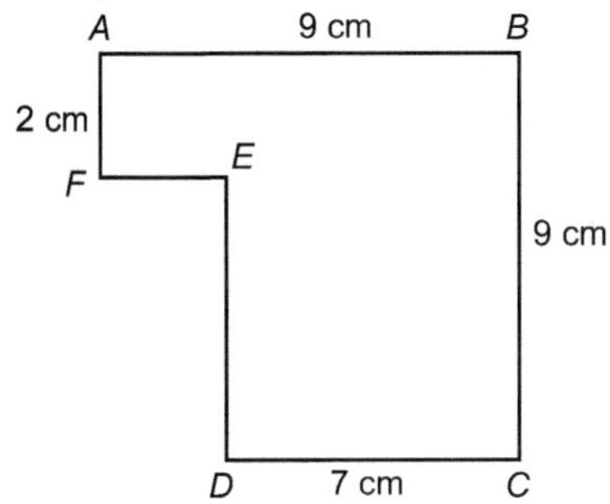

(a) 5 cm (b) 6 cm
(c) 7 cm (d) 8 cm

20. If the perimeter of a square is 56 cm. What is its area?
(a) 144 cm^2 (b) 196 cm^2
(c) 256 cm^2 (d) 324 cm^2

21. If the sides of a triangle are 17 cm, 15 cm, 8 cm, then what is the its area?
(a) 255 cm^2 (b) 60 cm^2
(c) 120 cm^2 (d) 136 cm^2

22. If the sides of a triangle are 12 cm, 16 cm, 18 cm, then what is its perimeter?
(a) 48 cm (b) 38 cm
(c) 42 cm (d) 46 cm

23. The area of square is 196 m^2. What is its perimeter?
(a) 44 m (b) 48 m
(c) 56 m (d) 64 m

24. The perimeter of a square is 24 cm. What is its diagonal?
(a) $3\sqrt{2}$ cm (b) $4\sqrt{2}$ cm
(c) $6\sqrt{2}$ cm (d) $8\sqrt{2}$ cm

25. What is the area of a triangle whose sides are, 3 cm, 4 cm and 5 cm?
(a) 12 cm^2 (b) 6 cm^2
(c) 8 cm^2 (d) 16 cm^2

26. The side of an equilateral triangle is $4\sqrt{3}$ cm. What is its area?
(a) $6\sqrt{3}$ cm^2 (b) $8\sqrt{3}$ cm^2
(c) $12\sqrt{3}$ cm^2 (d) $16\sqrt{3}$ cm^2

27. The area of an equilateral triangle is $\sqrt{3}$ m^2. What is its side?
(a) 1 m (b) 2 m
(c) 3 m (d) 4 m

28. The side of a rectangle is 4 m and its diagonal is 5 m. What is its area?
(a) 6 m^2 (b) 12 m^2
(c) 15 m^2 (d) 18 m^2

29. One side of a rectangle is 10 m and its diagonal is 26 m. What is its perimeter?
(a) 34 m (b) 44 m
(c) 48 m (d) 68 m

30. What is the perimeter of the given figure?

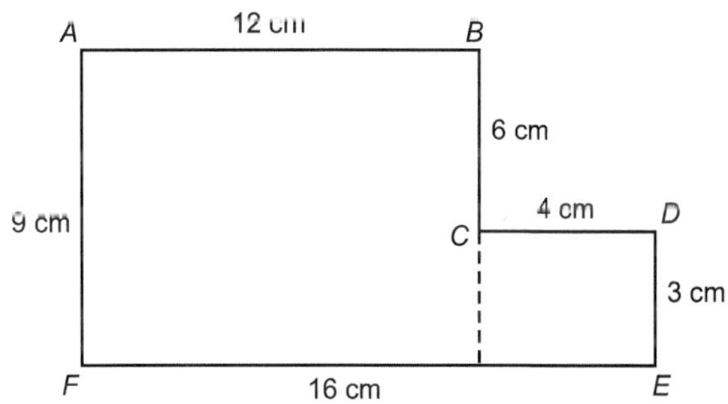

(a) 46 cm (b) 47 cm
(c) 48 cm (d) 50 cm

31. What is the area of above figure?
(a) 90 cm^2 (b) 96 cm^2
(c) 112 cm^2 (d) 120 cm^2

32. The length of rectangle is two times its breadth. If its area is 3200 m^2, then what is its breadth?
(a) 20 m (b) 30 m
(c) 40 m (d) 80 m

33. What is the area of circle whose radius is 14 cm?
(a) 516 cm^2 (b) 616 cm^2
(c) 716 cm^2 (d) None of these

34. What is the circumference of a circle whose diameter is 28 cm?
(a) 44 cm (b) 66 cm
(c) 88 cm (d) 176 cm

35. If area of a circle is 154 cm^2, then what is its radius?
(a) 6 cm (b) 7 cm
(c) 8 cm (d) 14 cm

36. The ratio of length and breadth of a rectangular field is 5 : 3 and its perimeter is 480 m. What is its area?
(a) 135 m^2 (b) 155 m^2
(c) 1550 m^2 (d) 13500 m^2

37. The area of a rectangular field is 396 m^2. If its length is 22 m, then what is its breadth?
(a) 16 m (b) 18 m
(c) 20 m (d) 24 m

38. The diagonal of a square is 6 metres. What is its area?
(a) 9 m^2 (b) 12 m^2
(c) 18 m^2 (d) 36 m^2

39. The circumference of a circle is 352 cm. What is its radius?
(a) 46 cm (b) 48 cm
(c) 56 cm (d) 58 cm

40. What will be the circumference of the circle whose radius is 21 cm?
(a) 132 cm (b) 146 cm
(c) 154 cm (d) 172 cm

41. What is the area of a triangle whose sides are 5 cm, 12 cm and 13 cm?
(a) 30 cm^2 (b) 60 cm^2
(c) 120 cm^2 (d) None of these

42. What will be the perimeter of a right angle triangle ABC, where $\angle B = 90°$, AB = $100\sqrt{3}$ cm and BC = 100 cm?
(a) $200\sqrt{3}$ (b) $300 + 100\sqrt{3}$
(c) $400\sqrt{3}$ (d) $100 + 100\sqrt{3}$

43. If the breadth of a rectangle is 8 m and its diagonal is 17 m. What is its perimeter?
(a) 42 cm (b) 44 cm
(c) 46 cm (d) 48 cm

44. What is the area of a circle whose circumference is 132 cm?
(a) 1284 cm^2 (b) 1384 cm^2
(c) 1286 cm^2 (d) 1386 cm^2

45. What will be the circumference of a circle if its area is 2464 cm^2?
(a) 176 cm (b) 88 cm
(c) 144 cm (d) 66 cm

46. Area of a square is 441 m^2. What is its perimeter?
(a) 64 m (b) 84 m
(c) 72 m (d) 92 m

47. The perimeter of a square is 68 cm. What is its area?
(a) 361 cm^2 (b) 269 cm^2
(c) 225 cm^2 (d) 289 cm^2

48. What is the perimeter of this figure?

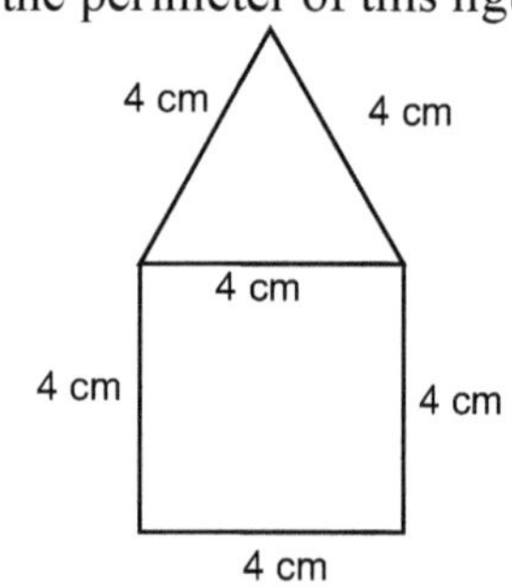

(a) 32 cm (b) 28 cm
(c) 26 cm (d) 20 cm

49. If diameter of a circle is 7 cm, then its circumference is
(a) 11 cm (b) 22 cm
(c) 33 cm (d) 44 cm

50. The perimeter of a triangle is 34 cm. If two of its sides are 12 cm and 14 cm. Then what is its third sides?
(a) 4 cm (b) 6 cm
(c) 8 cm (d) 10 cm

51. What is the perimeter of circle whose area is 1386 cm^2?
(a) 112 cm (b) 122 cm
(c) 124 cm (d) 132 cm

52. What is the diagonal of square whose area is 324 m^2?
(a) $9\sqrt{2}$ m (b) $12\sqrt{2}$ m
(c) $16\sqrt{2}$ m (d) $18\sqrt{2}$ m

53. What is the cost of fencing a rectangular field whose area is 960 m^2 and length is 48 m at the rate of ₹ 7 per meter?
(a) ₹ 952 (b) ₹ 962
(c) ₹ 972 (d) ₹ 942

54. The diagonal of a square field is $13\sqrt{2}$ cm. What is it perimeter?
(a) 52 cm (b) 48 cm
(c) 56 cm (d) 64 cm

55. The perimeter of a triangle is 56 cm. If two sides are 7 cm and 25 cm, then what is the area of triangle?
(a) 91 cm^2 (b) 92 cm^2
(c) 84 cm^2 (d) 96 cm^2

56. Area of a square is 1225 m^2. What is its perimeter?
(a) 160 m (b) 124 m
(c) 120 m (d) 140 m

57. What is the perimeter of semi-circle whose diameter is 56 cm?
(a) 134 cm (b) 144 cm
(c) 152 cm (d) 156 cm

58. The area of a rectangular hall is 750 m^2. If its breadth is 25 m, what is its perimeter?
(a) 100 m (b) 110 m
(c) 90 m (d) 120 m

59. The sides of a triangle are 7cm, 14 cm and 15 cm, then what is its area?
(a) $8\sqrt{66}$ cm^2 (b) $9\sqrt{66}$ cm^2
(c) $6\sqrt{33}$ cm^2 (d) $6\sqrt{66}$ cm^2

60. Area of an equilateral triangle is $16\sqrt{3}$ m^2. What is perimeter of triangle?
(a) 36 m (b) 18 m
(c) 32 m (d) 24 m

Darken Your Choice with HB Pencil

1.	ⓐ	ⓑ	ⓒ	ⓓ	13.	ⓐ	ⓑ	ⓒ	ⓓ	25.	ⓐ	ⓑ	ⓒ	ⓓ	37.	ⓐ	ⓑ	ⓒ	ⓓ	49.	ⓐ	ⓑ	ⓒ	ⓓ
2.	ⓐ	ⓑ	ⓒ	ⓓ	14.	ⓐ	ⓑ	ⓒ	ⓓ	26.	ⓐ	ⓑ	ⓒ	ⓓ	38.	ⓐ	ⓑ	ⓒ	ⓓ	50.	ⓐ	ⓑ	ⓒ	ⓓ
3.	ⓐ	ⓑ	ⓒ	ⓓ	15.	ⓐ	ⓑ	ⓒ	ⓓ	27.	ⓐ	ⓑ	ⓒ	ⓓ	39.	ⓐ	ⓑ	ⓒ	ⓓ	51.	ⓐ	ⓑ	ⓒ	ⓓ
4.	ⓐ	ⓑ	ⓒ	ⓓ	16.	ⓐ	ⓑ	ⓒ	ⓓ	28.	ⓐ	ⓑ	ⓒ	ⓓ	40.	ⓐ	ⓑ	ⓒ	ⓓ	52.	ⓐ	ⓑ	ⓒ	ⓓ
5.	ⓐ	ⓑ	ⓒ	ⓓ	17.	ⓐ	ⓑ	ⓒ	ⓓ	29.	ⓐ	ⓑ	ⓒ	ⓓ	41.	ⓐ	ⓑ	ⓒ	ⓓ	53.	ⓐ	ⓑ	ⓒ	ⓓ
6.	ⓐ	ⓑ	ⓒ	ⓓ	18.	ⓐ	ⓑ	ⓒ	ⓓ	30.	ⓐ	ⓑ	ⓒ	ⓓ	42.	ⓐ	ⓑ	ⓒ	ⓓ	54.	ⓐ	ⓑ	ⓒ	ⓓ
7.	ⓐ	ⓑ	ⓒ	ⓓ	19.	ⓐ	ⓑ	ⓒ	ⓓ	31.	ⓐ	ⓑ	ⓒ	ⓓ	43.	ⓐ	ⓑ	ⓒ	ⓓ	55.	ⓐ	ⓑ	ⓒ	ⓓ
8.	ⓐ	ⓑ	ⓒ	ⓓ	20.	ⓐ	ⓑ	ⓒ	ⓓ	32.	ⓐ	ⓑ	ⓒ	ⓓ	44.	ⓐ	ⓑ	ⓒ	ⓓ	56.	ⓐ	ⓑ	ⓒ	ⓓ
9.	ⓐ	ⓑ	ⓒ	ⓓ	21.	ⓐ	ⓑ	ⓒ	ⓓ	33.	ⓐ	ⓑ	ⓒ	ⓓ	45.	ⓐ	ⓑ	ⓒ	ⓓ	57.	ⓐ	ⓑ	ⓒ	ⓓ
10.	ⓐ	ⓑ	ⓒ	ⓓ	22.	ⓐ	ⓑ	ⓒ	ⓓ	34.	ⓐ	ⓑ	ⓒ	ⓓ	46.	ⓐ	ⓑ	ⓒ	ⓓ	58.	ⓐ	ⓑ	ⓒ	ⓓ
11.	ⓐ	ⓑ	ⓒ	ⓓ	23.	ⓐ	ⓑ	ⓒ	ⓓ	35.	ⓐ	ⓑ	ⓒ	ⓓ	47.	ⓐ	ⓑ	ⓒ	ⓓ	59.	ⓐ	ⓑ	ⓒ	ⓓ
12.	ⓐ	ⓑ	ⓒ	ⓓ	24.	ⓐ	ⓑ	ⓒ	ⓓ	36.	ⓐ	ⓑ	ⓒ	ⓓ	48.	ⓐ	ⓑ	ⓒ	ⓓ	60.	ⓐ	ⓑ	ⓒ	ⓓ

WORKBOOK

9 Geometrical Shapes and Angles

- Point is represented by a dot which has no length, breadth and height.
- A line passes through points but has no definite end points.
- Line segment is a portion of line having two end points.
- Angle is a figure consisting of two rays with a common initial point.

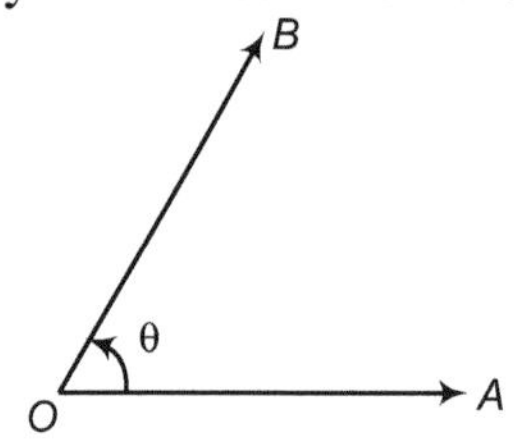

- Acute angle measures less than 90°.
  Example : 10°, 25°, 85°.

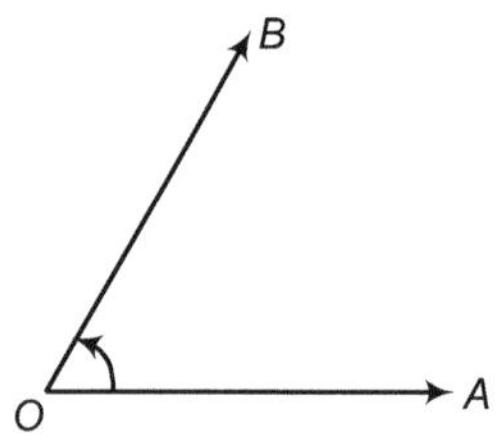

- A right angle measures 90°.

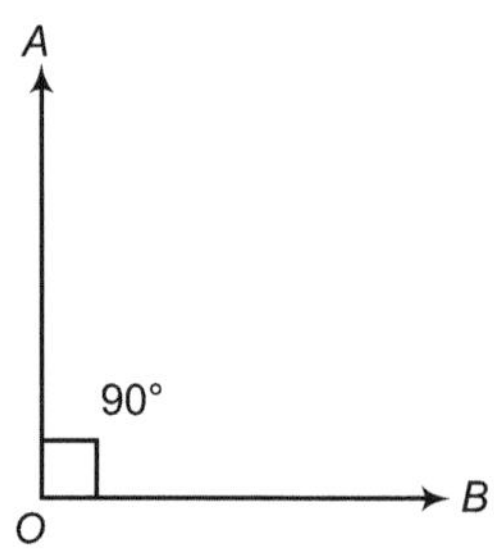

- Obtuse angle measures more than 90° and less than 180°.
  Example : 120°, 150°.

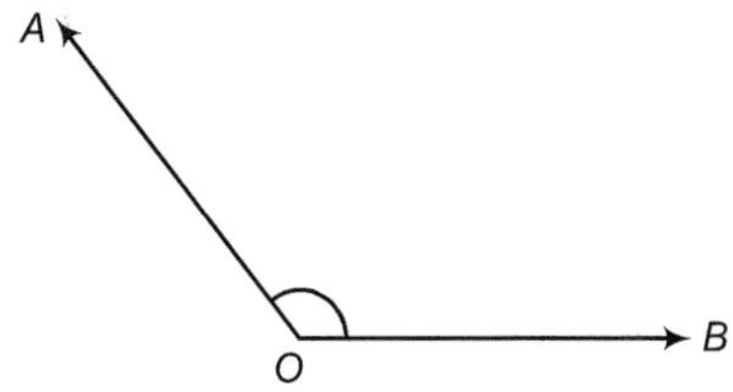

- **Straight Angle :** An angle whose measure is 180° is called a straight angle.

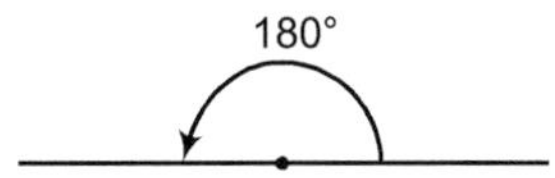

- Reflex angle is an angle whose measure is more than 180° and less than 360°.
  Example : 220°, 240° etc.

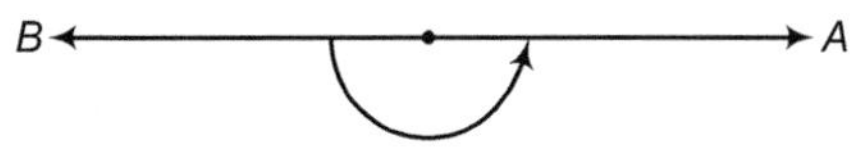

- **Complete angle :** An angle whose measure is 360° is called a complete angle.

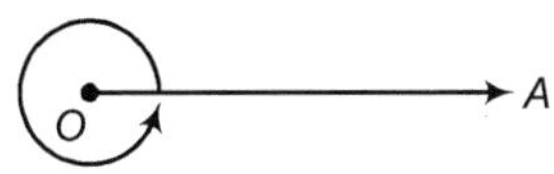

- Triangle is a closed figure consisting of three line segments linked end to end.

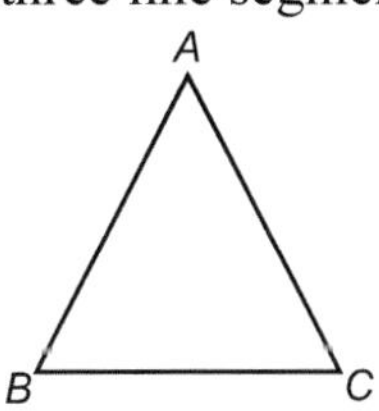

  The parts of triangles are vertices, base angles, altitude and median.
- **Scalene Triangle :** A triangle whose three sides are different in length.

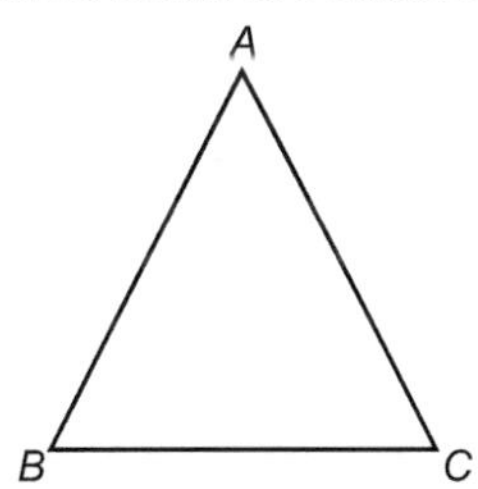

- **Isosceles Triangle :** A triangle which has two sides equal in length.

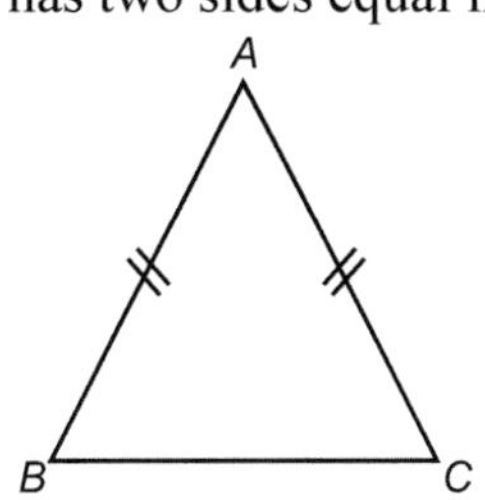

➟ **Equilateral Triangle :** A triangle which has all three sides equal in length.

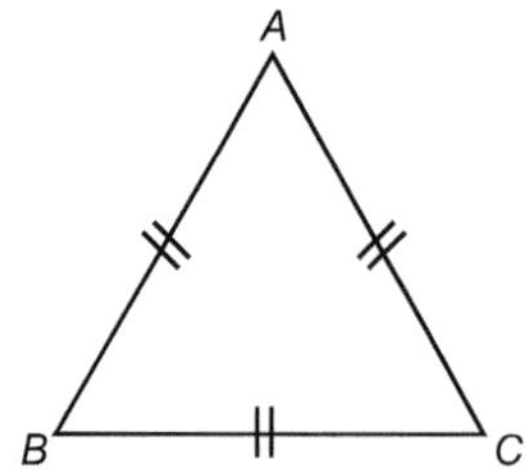

➟ **Right Triangle :** A triangle with one interior angle as 90°.

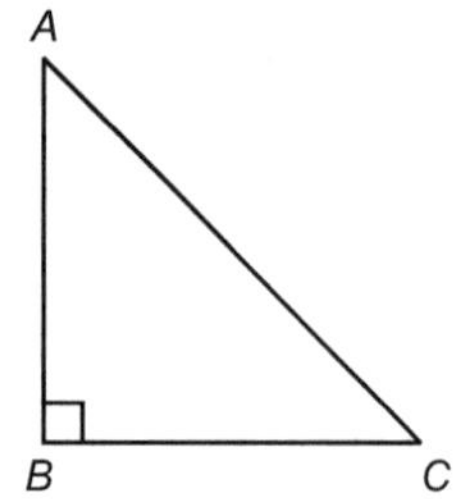

➟ **Obtuse Triangle :** A triangle with one of the interior angles greater than 90°.

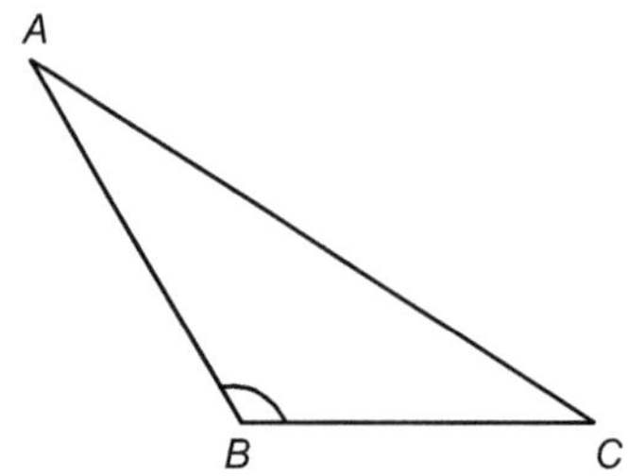

➟ **Acute Angle Triangle :** A triangle in which all three interior angles are acute, *i.e.*, less than 90°.

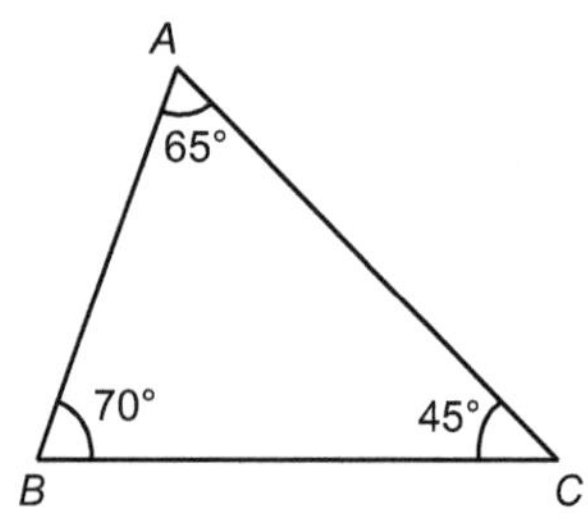

➟ A scalene right angle triangle has one right angle and two other unequal angles. No sides are equal.

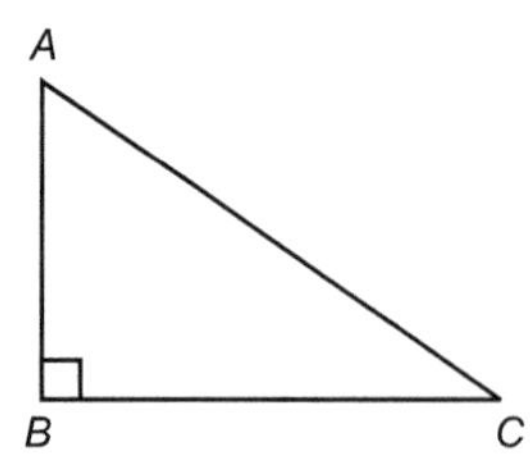

➠ **Isosceles right triangle** has one right angle, two equal sides and two equal angles of 45°.

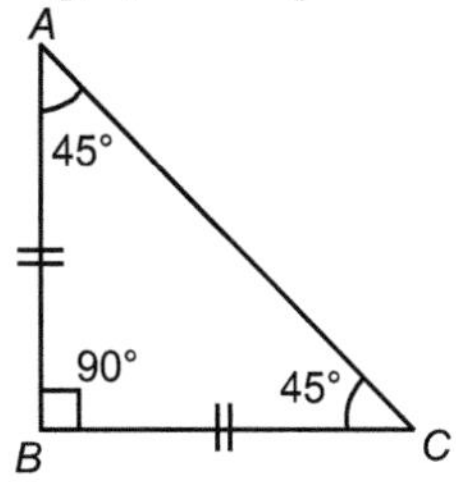

Multiple Choice Questions

1. Which of the following describes the triangle shown here?

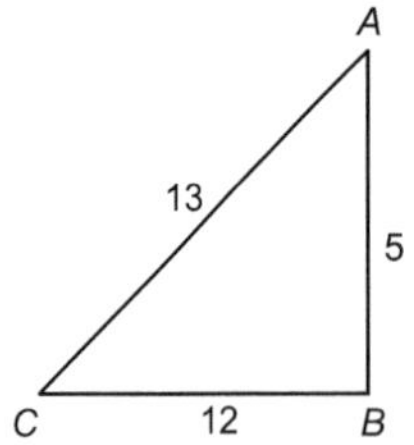

   (a) A scalene right angled triangle
   (b) A scalene acute angled triangle
   (c) A scalene obtuse angled triangle
   (d) An isosceles right angled triangle

2. Which of the following angles is not an obtuse angle?
   (a) 169° (b) 177°
   (c) 134° (d) 187°

3. Which of the following angles is not a reflex angle?
   (a) 179° (b) 183°
   (c) 275° (d) 351°

4. When two acute angles are added together then which of the following is not correct for their sum?
   (a) Right (b) Acute
   (c) Straight (d) Obtuse

5. Which of the following cannot be the sides of a triangle?
   (a) 3, 4, 7 (b) 3, 4, 5
   (c) 5, 12, 13 (d) 9, 8, 15

6. Which of the following cannot be the sides of a right angled triangle?
   (a) 3, 4, 5 (b) 5, 12, 13
   (c) 7, 15, 17 (d) 10, 24, 26

7. Which of the following is a complete angle?
   (a) 90° (b) 180°
   (c) 270° (d) 360°

8. Which of the following cannot be an angle of a triangle?
   (a) 97° (b) 87°
   (c) 103° (d) 180°

9. Which of the following cannot be an angle of a triangle?
   (a) 0° (b) 79°
   (c) 143° (d) 99°

10. The angle 98° is ________.
    (a) Acute (b) Obtuse
    (c) Right (d) Reflex

11. The angle 271° is ________.
    (a) Straight (b) Complete
    (c) Reflex (d) Obtuse

12. Which one of the following is an obtuse angle?
    (a) A right angle
    (b) Half a right angle
    (c) One and a half right angle
    (d) Two right angles

13. Which one of the following is a reflex angle?
    (a) Two right angles
    (b) One third of a complete angle
    (c) Three right angles
    (d) Four right angles

14. How many right angles make two full rotation?
    (a) 4 (b) 6
    (c) 8 (d) 10

15. How many straight angles are required to make one full rotation?
    (a) 1 (b) 2
    (c) 3 (d) 4

16. The sum of two angles is 320°. If one of the angles is reflex, the other angle cannot be ________.
    (a) Acute (b) Obtuse
    (c) Right (d) Reflex

17. The sides of a triangle are 9 cm, 7 cm, 16 cm. Which type of triangle is this?
    (a) Scalene (b) Right
    (c) Acute (d) None of these

18. The sides of a triangle are 5 cm, 13 cm and 12 cm. What is the type of triangle?
    (a) Right angle triangle

(b) Acute angle triangle
(c) Isosceles triangle
(d) Equilateral triangle

19. What is the measure of one angle of an equilateral triangle?
(a) 45° (b) 60°
(c) 90° (d) 120°

20. How many right angles may be there in a triangle?
(a) One (b) Two
(c) Three (d) None of these

21. Which of the following is not a reflex angle?
(a) 217° (b) 179°
(c) 312° (d) 297°

22. How many acute angles are there in this pentagram?

(a) 5 (b) 10 (c) 15 (d) 20

23. Which of the following angles is not acute?
(a) 67° (b) 3°
(c) 93° (d) 89°

24. The angle 237° is ________.
(a) Reflex (b) Obtuse
(c) Straight (d) Acute

25. The sum of 82° and 5° is which type of angle?
(a) Acute (b) Obtuse
(c) Right (d) None of these

26. When two obtuse angles are added, their sum cannot exceed ________.
(a) 180° (b) 270°
(c) 360° (d) None of these

27. Which of the following angles must be added to 137° so that their sum is a straight angle?
(a) 43° (b) 53°
(c) 33° (d) 63°

28. Which angle must be added to 59° so that their sum is a right angle?
(a) 21° (b) 31°
(c) 41° (d) None of these

29. Which of the following minimum angle must be added to 27° so that the sum is an obtuse angle?
(a) 64° (b) 63°
(c) 73° (d) 74°

30. The triangle with two sides equal is known as ________.
(a) Equilateral triangle
(b) Isosceles triangle
(c) Scalene triangle
(d) None of these

31. What will be the measure of angles in an isosceles right angled triangle?
(a) 90°, 60°, 30° (b) 90°, 55°, 35°
(c) 90°, 45°, 45° (d) 90°, 50°, 40°

32. How many right angles are there in a square?
(a) 2 (b) 3
(c) 4 (d) None of these

33. In the given figure, ∠AOB is closest to ________.

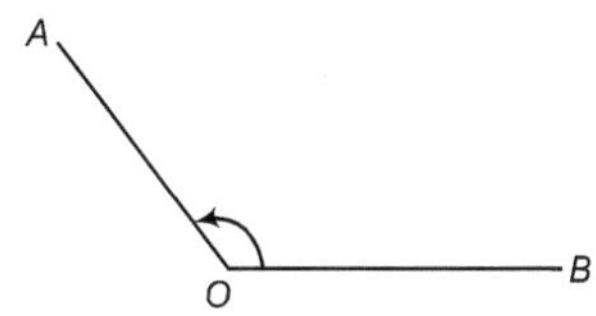

(a) 115° (b) 175°
(c) 180° (d) None of these

34. In the given figure, ∠XOY is closest to ________.

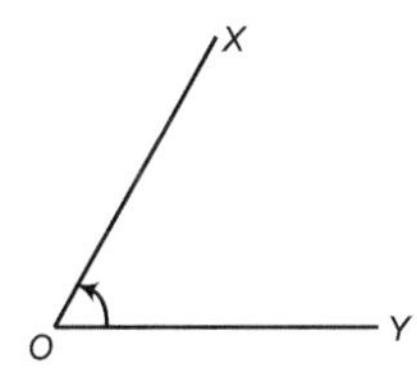

(a) 110° (b) 80°
(c) 160° (d) 15°

35. Which is closest to the size of reflex angle COD?

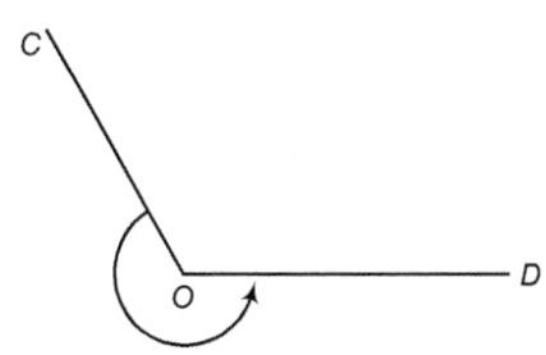

(a) 246° (b) 146°
(c) 186° (d) 206°

36. What is the maximum number of acute angles possible in a triangle?
 (a) 2 (b) 3
 (c) 1 (d) None of these

37. Which of the following cannot be an angle of a triangle?
 (a) 178° (b) 1°
 (c) 185° (d) None of these

38. What angle must be subtracted from 154° so that the difference will be a right angle?
 (a) 54° (b) 44°
 (c) 64° (d) 34°

39. How many lines can be drawn through a point?
 (a) One (b) Two
 (c) Three (d) Infinite

40. Two straight lines interest each other at how many points?
 (a) One (b) Two
 (c) Many (d) None of these

41. Which angle must be added to 297° to make it a complete angle?
 (a) 63° (b) 53°
 (c) 73° (d) 43°

42. Angle 203° is which type of angle?
 (a) Straight (b) Obtuse
 (c) Reflex (d) None of these

43. Angles of a parallelogram cannot be a ________.
 (a) Right angle (b) Acute angle
 (c) Obtuse angle (d) Reflex angle

44. What is complementary angle for 68°?
 (a) 22° (b) 32°
 (c) 42° (d) None of these

45. Two parallel lines meet at how many points?
 (a) One (b) Two
 (c) Three (d) None

46. Which of the following is correct for a triangle?
 (a) $a+b=c$ (b) $a+b<c$
 (c) $a+c>b$ (d) None of these

47. The angle 198° is ________.
 (a) Obtuse (b) Reflex
 (c) Straight (d) Right

48. Which of the following is the maximum that can be added to a right angle to make it obtuse?
 (a) 90 (b) 91
 (c) 89 (d) 75

49. How many straight angles make four full rotation?
 (a) 6 (b) 8
 (c) 10 (d) 12

50. How many right angles are there in 7 full rotation?
 (a) 14 (b) 16
 (c) 21 (d) 28

Darken Your Choice with HB Pencil

1.	ⓐ	ⓑ	ⓒ	ⓓ	11.	ⓐ	ⓑ	ⓒ	ⓓ	21.	ⓐ	ⓑ	ⓒ	ⓓ	31.	ⓐ	ⓑ	ⓒ	ⓓ	41.	ⓐ	ⓑ	ⓒ	ⓓ
2.	ⓐ	ⓑ	ⓒ	ⓓ	12.	ⓐ	ⓑ	ⓒ	ⓓ	22.	ⓐ	ⓑ	ⓒ	ⓓ	32.	ⓐ	ⓑ	ⓒ	ⓓ	42.	ⓐ	ⓑ	ⓒ	ⓓ
3.	ⓐ	ⓑ	ⓒ	ⓓ	13.	ⓐ	ⓑ	ⓒ	ⓓ	23.	ⓐ	ⓑ	ⓒ	ⓓ	33.	ⓐ	ⓑ	ⓒ	ⓓ	43.	ⓐ	ⓑ	ⓒ	ⓓ
4.	ⓐ	ⓑ	ⓒ	ⓓ	14.	ⓐ	ⓑ	ⓒ	ⓓ	24.	ⓐ	ⓑ	ⓒ	ⓓ	34.	ⓐ	ⓑ	ⓒ	ⓓ	44.	ⓐ	ⓑ	ⓒ	ⓓ
5.	ⓐ	ⓑ	ⓒ	ⓓ	15.	ⓐ	ⓑ	ⓒ	ⓓ	25.	ⓐ	ⓑ	ⓒ	ⓓ	35.	ⓐ	ⓑ	ⓒ	ⓓ	45.	ⓐ	ⓑ	ⓒ	ⓓ
6.	ⓐ	ⓑ	ⓒ	ⓓ	16.	ⓐ	ⓑ	ⓒ	ⓓ	26.	ⓐ	ⓑ	ⓒ	ⓓ	36.	ⓐ	ⓑ	ⓒ	ⓓ	46.	ⓐ	ⓑ	ⓒ	ⓓ
7.	ⓐ	ⓑ	ⓒ	ⓓ	17.	ⓐ	ⓑ	ⓒ	ⓓ	27.	ⓐ	ⓑ	ⓒ	ⓓ	37.	ⓐ	ⓑ	ⓒ	ⓓ	47.	ⓐ	ⓑ	ⓒ	ⓓ
8.	ⓐ	ⓑ	ⓒ	ⓓ	18.	ⓐ	ⓑ	ⓒ	ⓓ	28.	ⓐ	ⓑ	ⓒ	ⓓ	38.	ⓐ	ⓑ	ⓒ	ⓓ	48.	ⓐ	ⓑ	ⓒ	ⓓ
9.	ⓐ	ⓑ	ⓒ	ⓓ	19.	ⓐ	ⓑ	ⓒ	ⓓ	29.	ⓐ	ⓑ	ⓒ	ⓓ	39.	ⓐ	ⓑ	ⓒ	ⓓ	49.	ⓐ	ⓑ	ⓒ	ⓓ
10.	ⓐ	ⓑ	ⓒ	ⓓ	20.	ⓐ	ⓑ	ⓒ	ⓓ	30.	ⓐ	ⓑ	ⓒ	ⓓ	40.	ⓐ	ⓑ	ⓒ	ⓓ	50.	ⓐ	ⓑ	ⓒ	ⓓ

WORKBOOK

Logical Reasoning

PATTERN

- In the questions based on Pattern a set of figures and arrangement or a matrix is given, each of which has a certain character be it numbers, letters or a group or combination of letters or numbers. The candidate is required to analyse the pattern and find the missing character in the figure.
- In pattern the missing character is obtained by adding, subtracting, multiplying, or dividing by some number after going through the pattern. In the figure type, the middle term is the addition of all the given terms or addition of squares of each term or square of addition of all given terms.
- Sometimes the left part of figure has exactly the same relation as the right part of the figure. The candidate is required to find the certain rule to find the missing character. He/she should know various mathematical operations, squares, cubes, etc and relate them accordingly.

Example 1:

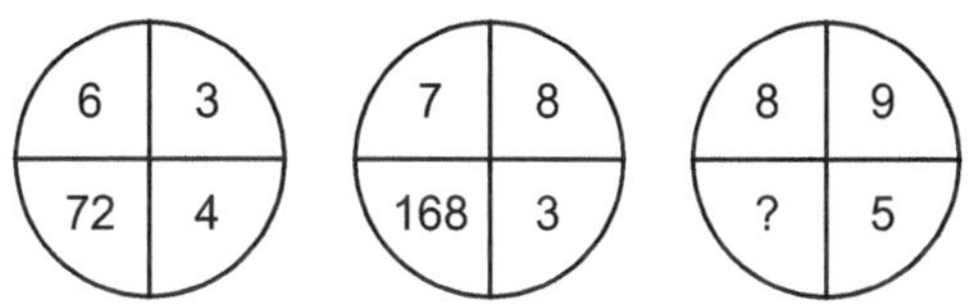

(a) 288 (b) 360 (c) 406 (d) 302

Ans. (b) : From Fig I. $6 \times 3 \times 4 = 72$

From Fig II. $7 \times 8 \times 3 = 168$

From Fig III. $8 \times 9 \times 5 = 360$

Example 2 :

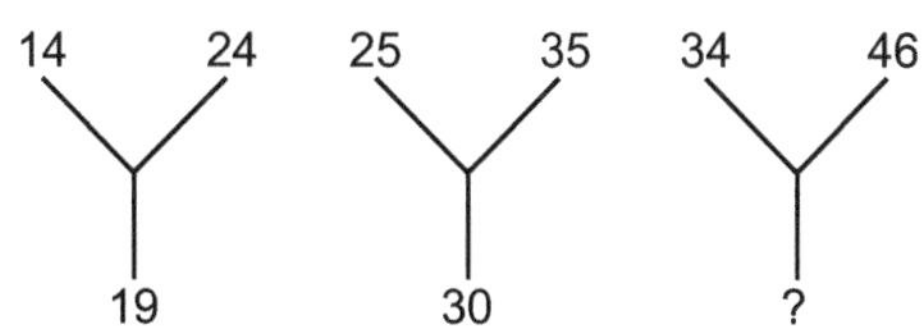

(a) 40 (b) 80 (c) 29 (d) 35

Ans. (a) : From Fig I. $(14 + 24) \div 2 = 38 \div 2 = 19$

From Fig II. $(25 + 35) \div 2 = 60 \div 2 = 30$

From Fig III. $(34 + 46) \div 2 = 80 \div 2 = 40$

ANALOGY

- Analogy means similarity. In the questions based on Analogy, two objects related in some way are given and a third object is also given with four or five alternatives. The student has to find out the alternative that bears the same relation with the third object as the first and second objects have.
- This type of questions covers all types of relationship that one can think of. There are many ways of establishing a relationship, some common ones are given here.

Example 1 : Cloth : Mill : : Newspaper : ?

(a) Editor (b) Reader

(c) Paper (d) Press

Ans. (d): As cloth is made in a mill, similarly newspaper is printed in press.

Example 2 : Cassock : Priest : : ? : Graduate

(a) Cap (b) Tie

(c) Coat (d) Gown

Ans. (d): A priest wears cassock while graduate wears gown.

Example 3 : 24 : 60 : : 120 : ?

(a) 160 (b) 220

(c) 300 (d) 108

Ans. (c): As 24 : 60 = (2/5)

Similarly, (120/300) = 2/5

Example 4 : DIRGE : FUNERAL

(a) Chain : Letter (b) Bell : Church

(c) Telephone : Call (d) Jingle : Commercial

Ans. (d): A dirge is song sung at funeral; a jingle is a song sung in commercial.

NUMBER AND RANKING TEST

- The problems based on number ranking consist of a set, group or series of numerals. The candidate has to trace out the numerals following some certain given conditions or lying at particular specified position according to a certain given pattern. For this, he/she has to analyse the given series of numerals or number sequence and study the pattern to answer the appropriate option.
- **Number Test :** In this type of questions a series of numbers is given. The students have to study the series and answer the given questions according to given conditions.
- **Ranking Test :** In this test the rank of a person from the top and from the bottom is mentioned and the candidate has to find out the total number of persons.
- In some problems the test is in the form of puzzle of interchanging positions by two persons. In the ranking problems, the student has to find out the total number of persons, position of particular person from left end or right end.

Example 1 : Rahul ranks 16th in a class of 80 students. What in his rank from last?

(a) 63 (b) 64 (c) 62 (d) 65

Ans. (d) : Here, 80 – 16 = 64

So, Rahul's rank = 64 + 1 = 65th from the last.

Example 2 : Suresh is 10 ranks ahead of Mukesh in a class of 80. If Mukesh's rank is 17th from the last, what is Suresh's rank from the start?

(a) 70 (b) 45 (c) 44 (d) 46

Ans. (c) : Mukesh's rank is 17th from the last.

Suresh's rank 17 + 10 = 27th from the last.

No. of students ahead of Suresh = 80 – 27 = 43

Suresh's rank from start = 43 + 1 = 44th

MIRROR IMAGES

➠ **Mirror Image :** The image of an object as seen in a mirror is called its mirror reflection or mirror image.

In such an image, the right side of the object appears to be on the left and viceversa, therefore said to be laterally inverted and the phenomenon is called lateral inversion.

Mirror Image of Capital Letters

Letter	Mirror Image	Letter	Mirror Image	Letter	Mirror Image
A	A	J	Ⴑ	S	Ƨ
B	ᗺ	K	ꓘ	T	T
C	Ɔ	L	⅃	U	U
D	ᗡ	M	M	V	V
E	Ǝ	N	И	W	W
F	ꟻ	O	O	X	X
G	Ә	P	ꟼ	Y	Y
H	H	Q	Ϙ	Z	Σ
I	I	R	Я	–	

Mirror Image of Small Letters

Letter	Mirror Image	Letter	Mirror Image	Letter	Mirror Image
a	ɒ	j	į	s	ƨ
b	d	k	ʞ	t	ƚ
c	ɔ	l	l	u	u
d	b	m	m	v	v
e	ɘ	n	n	w	w
f	ʇ	o	o	x	x
g	ϱ	p	q	y	γ
h	ᖹ	q	p	z	ƹ
i	i	r	ɿ	–	–

Mirror Images of Numbers

Number	Mirror image	Number	Mirror image	Number	Mirror image
1	I	4	ᔨ	7	Ꞁ
2	ƨ	5	ꙅ	8	8
3	Ɛ	6	∂	9	ϱ

Choose the alternative which most clearly resembles the mirror image of the given combination.

Example 1 : TARAIN1014A

(a) AᔨꓕOIИIAЯAꓕ

(b) AI0IᔨИIAЯAT

(c) AI0ꓕᔨTAЯAIИ

(d) AᔨI0IИIAЯAT

Ans. (d): TARAINI1014A → AᔨI0IИIAЯAT

Example 2 : JUDGEMENT

(a) TNEMEGDUJ

(b) TИƎMƎƆDUႱ

(c) TИƎMƎӘᗡUႱ

(d) ႱUᗡӘƎMƎИT

Ans. (c): JUDGEMENT → TИƎMƎӘᗡUႱ

ALPHABET TEST

Alphabetical order means arrangement of words as they appear in the English dictionary. This is the order in which the beginning letters of these words appear in the English alphabet. First, consider the first letter of each word, then second and so on and then arrange the words in the order in which the letters appear in English alphabet.

Example 1 : Arrange the given words in alphabetical order.

Tiger, File, Priest, Cricket, Basketball, Finger.

The order of words as per English dictionary is as follows :

Basketball, Cricket, File, Finger, Priest, Tiger

Arranging words in alphabetical order implies 'to arrange them in the order as they appear in a dictionary', *i.e.*, as per the order in which the beginning letters of these words appear in the English alphabet.

Directions (2–4) : Arrange the given words in alphabetical order and choose the one that comes first.

Example 2 :

(a) Fire (b) Final (c) File (d) Fixed

Ans. (c): File, Final, Fire, Fixed

Example 3 :

(a) Eat (b) Egg (c) Eagle (d) Ear

Ans. (c): Eagle, Ear, Eat, Egg

Example 4 :

(a) Toffee (b) Toy (c) Toe (d) Toilet

Ans. (c): Toe, Toffee, Toilet, Toy.

Example 5 : Number of letters skipped in between adjacent letters decrease in order.

(a) SYDHK (b) HNSWA

(c) AGMRV (d) NSXCH

Ans. (a): @ [S] T U V W X [Y] Z A B C [D] E F G [H] I J [K].

CODING–DECODING

- A code is a system of signals. Therefore, coding is a method of transmitting a message between the sender and the receiver without a third person knowing it.
- The coding and decoding test is set up to judge the candidate's ability to decipher the rule that codes a particular word/message and break the code to decipher the message.

Example 1 : In a certain system of coding, the word PERMANENT is written as TIVQERIRX, How is POLLUTION written in the same code?

(a) TSPPYXMSW (b) TSPPXYWSM (c) STPPYXMSW (d) TSXXPYMSW

Ans. (a) : POLLUTION $\xrightarrow{+4}$ T S P P Y X M S W

- **Direct Letter Coding :** Letters are assigned codes according to a set pattern or rule concerning the movement or reordering of letters and one needs to detect this hidden rule to decode a message.
- Such type of coding is called direct coding. The code letters occur in the same sequence as the corresponding letters occur in the words.
- **Number/symbol coding :** Numerical code values are assigned to a word or alphabetical code letters are assigned to the numbers. Letters and numbers are correlated to each other in no other way except in relation to the position of the letters in the English alphabet.

Example 2 : If NOIDA is written as 39658, how will INDIA be written?

(a) 36568 (b) 65368 (c) 63568 (d) 63563

Ans. (c) :

Letter : N O I D A
Code : 3 9 6 5 8

Letter : I N D I A
Code : 6 3 5 6 8

PUZZLE TEST

- The questions based on figure puzzles are designed to test candidate's skills in mathematical operations and numbers.
- In mathematical operations, usual mathematical symbols are converted into another form by either interchanging the symbols or using different symbols in place of original symbols in order to make simple calculation tedious.
- On the other hand, in the questions asked on number puzzles a few numbers are inserted into a figure which follows a particular rule for the placement of different numbers at different places.
- Students are asked to select the missing number following the rule of placement of numbers from the given options.

Example 1 : Which one will replace the question mark.

4	7	5
33	78	46
8	11	?

(a) 11 (b) 10 (c) 12 (d) 9

Ans. (d) : From column I $(4 \times 8) + 1 = 33$

From column II $(7 \times 11) + 1 = 78$

From column III $(5 \times ?) + 1 = 46$

$$? = \frac{45}{5} = 9$$

Example 2 : Which one will replace the question mark?

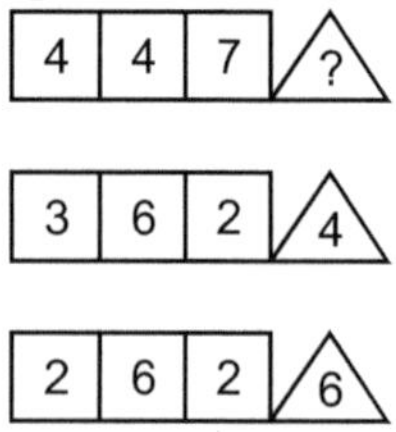

(a) 7 (b) 8 (c) 2 (d) 10

Ans. (a) : Row I $(4 \times 7) \div 4 = \boxed{7}$

Row II $(6 \times 2) \div 3 = 4$

Row III $(6 \times 2) \div 2 = 6$

DIRECTION SENSE TEST

- The questions on direction sense are based on various directions called direction puzzles. The figure given below shows four main directions namely North, South, East and West. There are four cardinal directions namely North-East (NE), North-West (NW), South-East (SE) and South-West (SW).

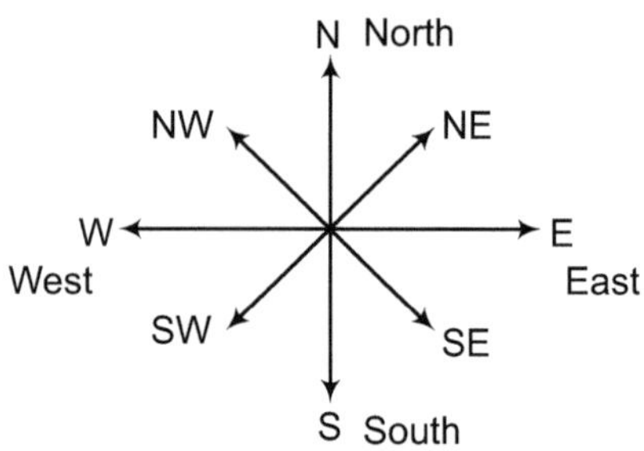

- In this type of questions a successive follow up of directions is formulated. The candidate is required to decide the final direction or distance between starting and end points. Direction sense test basically checks the candidate's ability to trace and follow the direction correctly.
- The candidate is required to trace the diagram and find out the distance between initial point and final point. He/She has to analyse directions carefully and answer the questions. The diagram is very essential in direction sense problems.

Example 1 : Tinku walks 40 m towards south, then turning to his right walks 40 m, then turns left and walks 20 m. Again he turns to his left and walks 40 m. How far is he from his starting position?

(a) 30 m (b) 40 m (c) 50 m (d) 60 m

Ans. (d) : The movements of Tinku are as shown below :

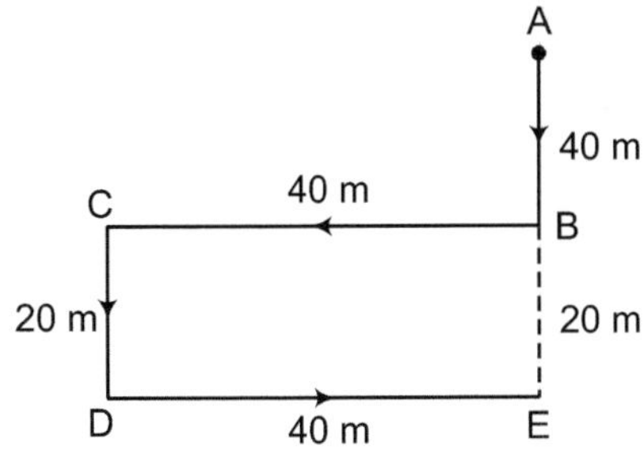

Starting point A, final point E.

$$AE = AB + BE = AB + CD = 40 + 20 = 60 \text{ m}$$

Example 2 : Mukesh walks 30 m towards south. Then turning to his right, he walks 30 m then turning to his left, he walks 20 m. Again he turns to his left and walks 30 m. How far is he from his initial position?

(a) 30 m (b) 40 m (c) 50 m (d) 60 m

Ans. (c) : The movements of Mukesh are as shown in the given figure.

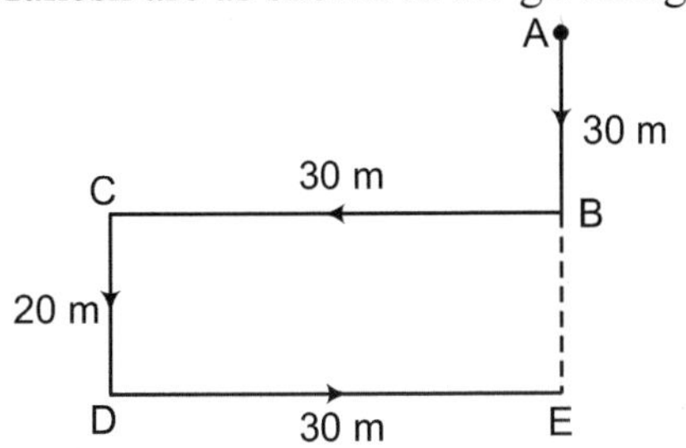

∴ Mukesh's distance from initial position A

$= AE = (AB + BE) = (AB + CD)$

$= (30 + 20) \text{ m} = 50 \text{ m}$

WATER IMAGES

- The reflection of an object as seen in water is called its water image. It is the inverted image obtained by turning the object upside down.

Water Image of Capital Letters

Letter	A	B	C	D	E	F	G	H	I
Water Image	∀	B	C	D	E	Ⅎ	⅁	H	I
Letter	J	K	L	M	N	O	P	P	R
Water Image	ſ	K	Γ	W	И	O	b	b	ꓤ
Letter	S	T	U	V	W	X	Y	Z	—
Water Image	Ƨ	⊥	∩	Λ	M	X	⅄	Σ	—

Water Image of Small Letters

Letter	a	b	c	d	e	f	g	h	i
Water Image	ɐ	p	c	q	ǝ	ʈ	ƃ	ɥ	!
Letter	j	k	l	m	n	o	p	q	r
Water Image	ɾ	ʞ	l	ɯ	u	o	b	d	ɹ
Letter	s	t	u	v	w	x	y	z	—
Water Image	s	ʇ	n	ʌ	ʍ	x	λ	z	—

Water Image of Numbers

Letter	0	1	2	3	4	5	6	7	8	9
Water Image	0	I	Ƨ	3	ᔭ	ટ	ɑ	⅃	8	ə

Example1 : Choose the alternative which closely resembles the water image of the given combination.

CODE

(a) CODE (b) EDOC (c) ƆOᗡƎ (d) ƆODƎ

Ans. (a)

CLASSIFICATION

- Classification means to analyse the items of a given group on the basis of certain common properties they posses and then mark the odd one. In this type of questions, a group of certain items are given out of which all except one are similar to one another in some manner. We have to choose the odd one, which is not suitable for the given group. There are mainly three types of questions.
- **Type I :** Choosing the odd word which is different from the other three.

  Example 1: Choose the odd one out.

  (a) Brother (b) Mother (c) Sister (d) Aunt

  Ans. (a): Except brother, all others are females.

  Example 2: Choose the odd one out.

  (a) Rhombus (b) Square (c) Triangle (d) Rectangle

  Ans. (c) Except c, all others have four sides.
- **Type II :** Choosing the odd numeral.

  In this type, four numbers are given, out of the these numbers all except one have some common properties.

Example 3:

(a) 443 (b) 551 (c) 782 (d) 967

Ans. (c): Except 782, all others are odd numbers.

- **Type III :** Choosing the odd pair of words. In this type, four pairs of words are given. All pairs except one have some common relationship. We have to choose the odd one.

Example 4 :

(a) Pen : Pencil (b) Shovel : Mud

(c) Hammer : Nail (d) Screw driver : Screw

Ans. (a): In all pairs, the first is a tool which works on the second.

Example 5 :

(a) Loom : Cloth (b) Table : Drawer

(c) Book : Page (d) Car : Wheel

Ans. (a): In all other pairs, the second is part of the first.

Multiple Choice Questions

1. Tobacco is related to Nerves in the same way as alcohol is related to ______.
(a) Liver (b) Liquor
(c) Head (d) Intoxication

2. Book is related to magazine in the same way as Newspaper is related to ______.
(a) Headline (b) Article
(c) News (d) Journal

3. Thick is related to thin in the same way as idle is related to ______.
(a) Industrious (b) Active
(c) Business (d) Virtuous

4. Satyajit Ray is related to film in the same way Picasso is related to ______.
(a) Literature (b) Poetry
(c) Painting (d) Drama

5. Charminar is related to India in the same way as Sphinx is related to ______.
(a) Egypt (b) Vetican
(c) Canada (d) England

6. Umbrella is related to rain in the same way as goggles is related to ______.
(a) Sight (b) Glass
(c) Stare (d) Light

7. Face is related to expression in the same way as hand is related to ______.
(a) Waving (b) Work
(c) Handshake (d) Gesture

8. Writer is related to reader in the same way as producer is related to ______.
(a) Contractor (b) Creator
(c) Seller (d) Consumer

9. England is related to Atlantic ocean in the same way as Greenland is related to ______.
(a) Antarctic Ocean (b) Atlantic Ocean
(c) Pacific Ocean (d) Arctic Ocean

Direction (10-19) : Find the odd one from the following.

10. (a) Kiwi (b) Ostrich
(c) Eagle (d) Penguine

11. (a) Rectangle (b) Square
(c) Cube (d) Triangle

12. (a) Correction (b) Improvement
(c) Betterment (d) Elevation

13. (a) Rain (b) Mist
(c) Fog (d) Smoke

14. (a) Himadri (b) Shivalik
(c) Kanla (d) Himachal

15. (a) Wood (b) Cork
(c) Stone (d) Paper

16. (a) Ballot (b) Manifesto
(c) Election (d) Vote

17. (a) Owl (b) Eagle
(c) Hawk (d) Parrot

18. (a) Herb (b) Flower
(c) Tree (d) Shrub

19. (a) Circle (b) Ellipse
(c) Sphere (d) Cube

Direction (20-25) : Choose the odd numeral from the following questions.

20. (a) 121 (b) 144
(c) 179 (d) 196

21. (a) 112 (b) 118
(c) 126 (d) 115

22. (a) 127 (b) 291
(c) 328 (d) 471

23. (a) 101 (b) 103
(c) 105 (d) 107

24. (a) 27 (b) 64
(c) 126 (d) 216

25. (a) 361 (b) 625
(c) 576 (d) 677

Direction (26-29) : Arrange the given words in alphabetical order and choose the one which comes first.

26. (a) Crowd (b) Cruel
(c) Crown (d) Crockery

27. (a) Proud (b) Pleasure
(c) Penalty (d) Pendulum

28. (a) Naughty (b) Narrate
(c) Nature (d) Native

29. (a) Particle (b) Passion
(c) Partition (d) Parlour

Direction (30–33) : Arrange the given words in alphabetical order and choose the one which comes last.

30. (a) Legal (b) Lenient
(c) Length (d) Legible

31. (a) Bonafide (b) Bottle
(c) Blast (d) Bondage

32. (a) Similar (b) Stimulate
(c) Summary (d) Skeleton

33. (a) Temperature (b) Terminate
(c) Tenacious (d) Temple

34. Which letter is on the sixth position from the right end in English alphabet?
(a) U (b) V
(c) T (d) S

35. Which letter is the 19th position from the left end in English alphabet?
(a) S (b) T
(c) R (d) U

36. Which letter is fifth to the right of eighteenth letter from right end of alphabet?
(a) M (b) L
(c) N (d) P

37. Which letter is in the exact middle between D and L?
(a) G (b) H
(c) I (d) F

38. If English alphabet is written in reverse order then which letter is 11th from left end?
(a) P (b) Q
(c) R (d) N

39. How many odd numbers are there in the series each of which is immediately in between even numbers?
465725817642658352165739
(a) 1 (b) 2
(c) 3 (d) 4

40. In the given series, how many 6's are there, which is in between 5 and 7?
7542685674324868567134982
(a) 1 (b) 2
(c) 3 (d) 4

41. Ankush ranks 12th in a class of 90 students. What is his rank from last?
(a) 78 (b) 77
(c) 79 (d) 80

42. Sumit ranks 11th from top and 66th from bottom. How many students are there in the class?
(a) 75 (b) 76
(c) 74 (d) 78

43. Rohit's rank is 7th in 55 students. What is his rank from last?
(a) 47th (b) 48th
(c) 49th (d) 50th

44. In the given series how many 7's are there, which are in between two even numbers?
8456781235762374587432567
(a) 1 (b) 2
(c) 3 (d) 4

45. In the given series how many 9's are there, which are in between 7 and 5?
2489367952463459782463
(a) 1 (b) 2
(c) 3 (d) 4

Direction (46-56) : Complete the given series.

46. 127, 140, 155, 172, 191, 212, ?
(a) 225 (b) 235
(c) 237 (d) 245

47. 15, 31, 63, 127, 255, 511, ?
(a) 1019 (b) 1021
(c) 1027 (d) 1023

48. 117, 142, 167, 192, 217, 242, 267, ?
(a) 289 (b) 292
(c) 291 (d) 293

49. 17, 51, 153, 459, 1377, ?
(a) 4031 (b) 4131
(c) 3931 (d) 4231

50. 7, 8, 18, 57, 232, 1165, ?
(a) 6946 (b) 6976
(c) 6986 (d) 6996

51. 9, 27, 108, 540, ?
(a) 2940 (b) 3120
(c) 3140 (d) 3240

52. 325, 436, 547, 658, ?
(a) 769 (b) 768
(c) 767 (d) 766

53. 907, 850, 793, 736, 679, ?
(a) 619 (b) 621
(c) 622 (d) 623

54. 7, 9, 16, 25, 41, 66, 107, ?
(a) 171 (b) 172
(c) 173 (d) 174

55. 2, 5, 12, 27, 58, ?
(a) 119 (b) 121
(c) 123 (d) 125

56. 4, 7, 16, 43, 124, ?
(a) 364 (b) 365
(c) 366 (d) 367

57. In a certain code 'TEACHER' is coded as 'UFBDIFS'. How is 'MOUNTAIN' coded in that code?
(a) NPVOUBJO (b) NPVPUBK
(c) NPVOVBJO (d) None of these

58. If DIAMOND is coded as FKCOQPF, then what is code for WEALTH?
(a) YGBNUK (b) YFCNUJ
(c) YGBNVJ (d) YGCNVJ

59. If DISTURB is coded as EKTVVTC, then what is the code for FRANTIC?
(a) GTCPUKD (b) GTBPUKD
(c) GSBPUKD (d) None of these

60. If TAJMAHAL is coded as SZILZGZK, then what is code for QUTABMINAR?
(a) PTSZALHMZQ
(b) PTSBCMHMZQ
(c) PRSZALHMZQ
(d) PTSZANHMBQ

61. If HUMIDITY is coded as IVNJEJUZ, then how POLITICS is coded in that code?
(a) QPMLUJDT (b) QPMKUJDT
(c) QPMKVJDT (d) QPMJUJDT

62. If GOLD is coded as IQNF, then how is WIND coded in that code?
(a) YKPF (b) XKPF
(c) YKPE (d) YJPE

63. If PROBLEM is coded as MELBORP, then what is code for NUMBERS?
(a) NUMSREB (b) SREBMUN
(c) NUMREBS (d) MUNBERS

64. If South West is called South, North-West is called West, South-East is called East and so on. What will North be called?
(a) East (b) South
(c) North-West (d) North-East

65. Ankush travels 30 km towards East, then took a right turn and travels 40 km. Then he took a left turn and travelled 30 km. In which direction is he now with respect to the starting point?
(a) South (b) East
(c) North-East (d) South-East

66. Lalit went 15 km to the West from his house, then turned left and covered 20 km. He then turned towards East and covered 25 km and finally turning left he covered 20 km. How far was he from his house?
(a) 10 km (b) 20 km
(c) 30 km (d) 40 km

67. Arman is facing North-West. He turns 90° in clockwise direction and then 135° in anti clockwise direction. In which direction is he facing now?
(a) East (b) West
(c) North (d) South

68. Jay went 25 km to the West from his house then turned left and walked 20 km. He then turned towards East and walked 45 km. At last, by turning left he walked 20 km. How far is he from his house?
(a) 5 km (b) 10 km
(c) 15 km (d) 20 km

69. Sonal is 40 m South-West of Ravi. Salman is to the East of Ravi, then Salman is in which direction of Sonal?
(a) South (b) North-East
(c) West (d) East

70. Going 70 m to the South of his house Monu turns left and covers 20 m, then he turns towards North and covers 40 m and starts

walking to his house. In which direction is he walking now?

(a) South-East (b) North-West

(c) East (d) West

Direction (71–86) : Choose the correct mirror image of the figure in (X).

71. 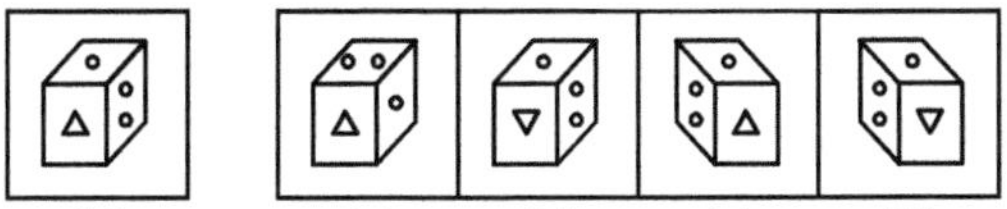

(X) (a) (b) (c) (d)

72. 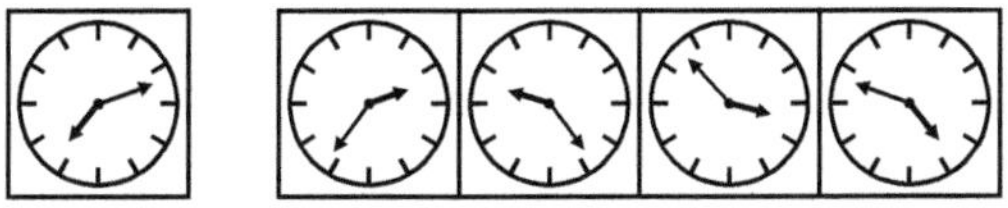

(X) (a) (b) (c) (d)

73. 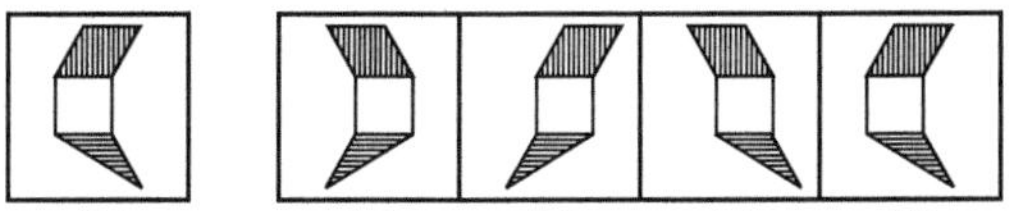

(X) (a) (b) (c) (d)

74. 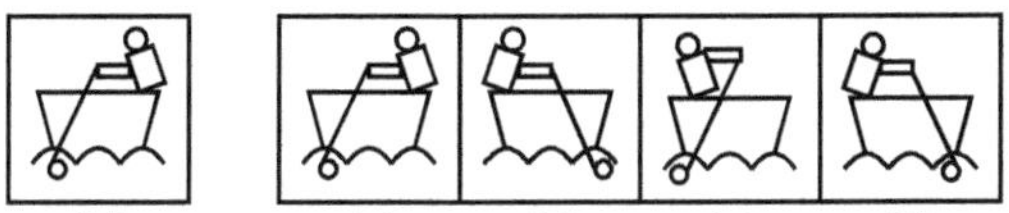

(X) (a) (b) (c) (d)

75. 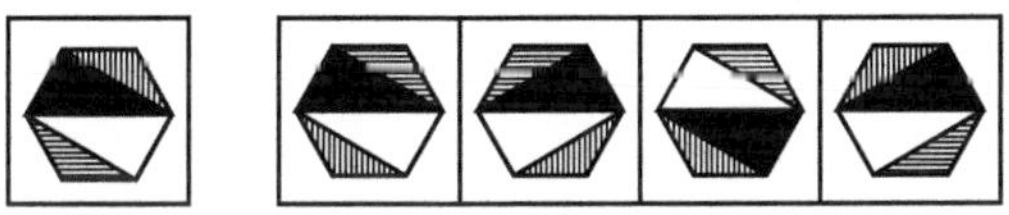

(X) (a) (b) (c) (d)

76. 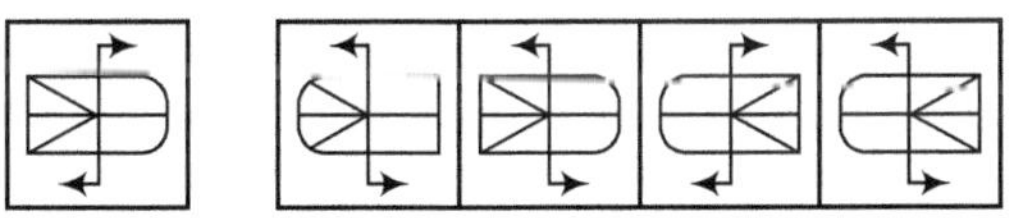

(X) (a) (b) (c) (d)

77. 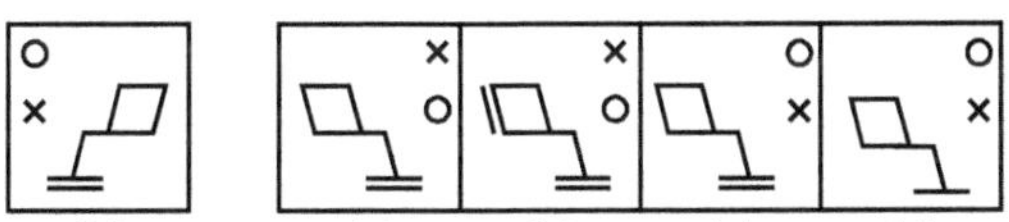

(X) (a) (b) (c) (d)

78. 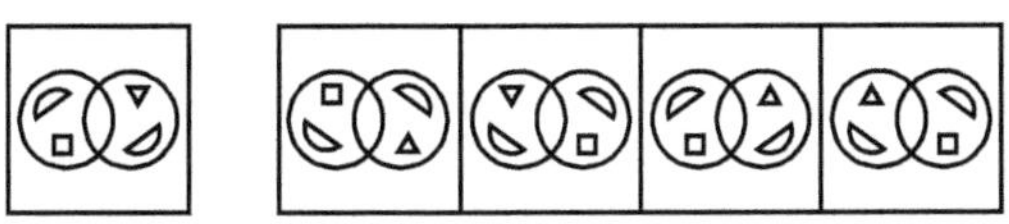

(X) (a) (b) (c) (d)

79. 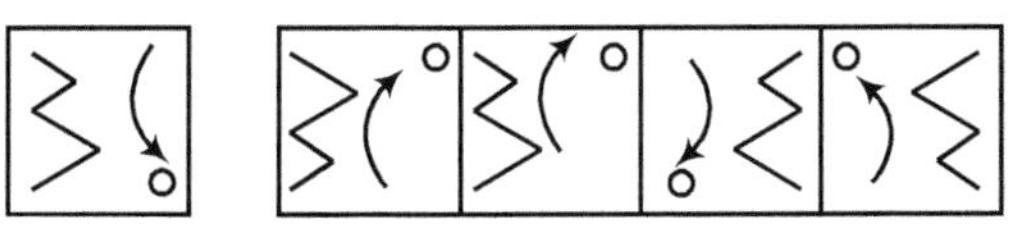

(X) (a) (b) (c) (d)

80. 

(X) (a) (b) (c) (d)

81. 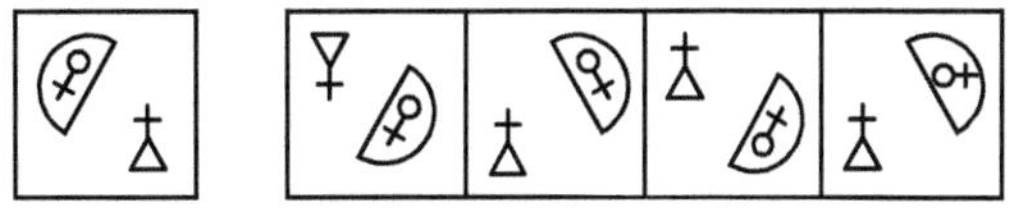

(X) (a) (b) (c) (d)

82. 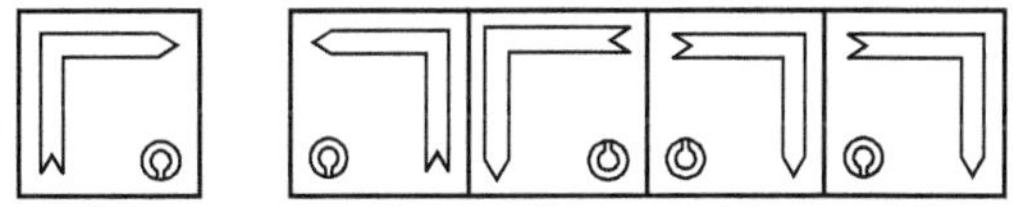

(X) (a) (b) (c) (d)

83. 

(X) (a) (b) (c) (d)

84. 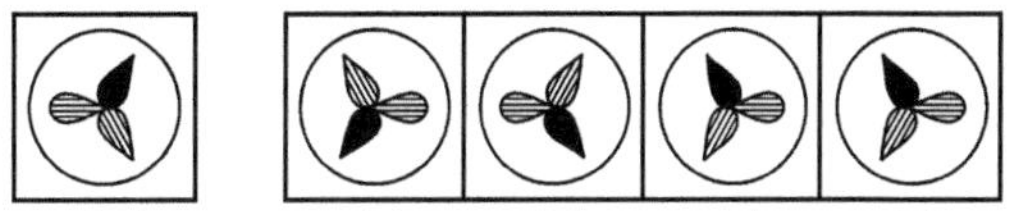

(X) (a) (b) (c) (d)

85. 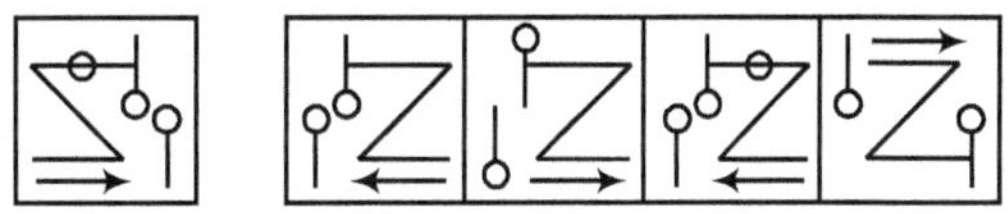

(X) (a) (b) (c) (d)

86. 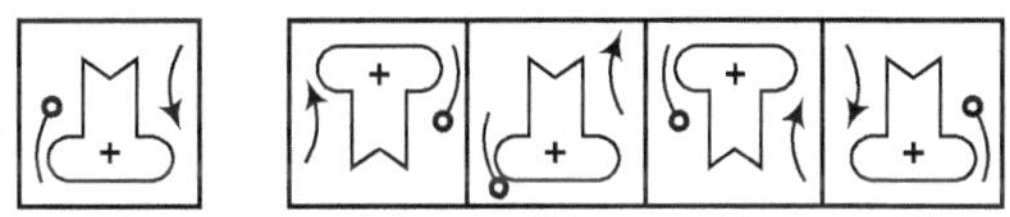

(X) (a) (b) (c) (d)

Direction (87–100) : Choose the correct water image of the given word.

87. QUESTION

(a) ϬՈΕƧΤΙΟͶ (b) ИOITƧƎUϘ

(c) NOITSEUQ (d) NOITSƎUϘ

88. SURFACE

(a) ƎƆⱯℲЯՈƧ (b) ƎƆAᖷЯUƧ

(c) ƧUЯᖷAƆƎ (d) ƧՈᴚℲⱯƆE

89. EXPOSE

(a) ESOPXE (b) EXPOSE

(c) EXbOƧE (d) EPOSXE

90. DISCLOSE

(a) ƎSO⅃ƆSIᗡ (b) DIƧϹΓOƧE

(c) ESOLCSID (d) ƎƧO⅃ϽƧIᗡ

91. OBLITERATE
(a) ETARETILBO (b) OBLITEꓤⱯTE
(c) EBLITERATO (d) ƎTAЯƎTI⅃ᙠO

92. TERMINATE
(a) ƎTAИIMЯƎT (b) TEꓤMIИⱯTE
(c) ꓕEꓤMIИⱯꓕE (d) ƎTAИIMЯƎꓕ

93. STRAIN
(a) ИIⱯЯꓕƧ (b) ƧTЯAIИ
(c) ИIⱯЯTƧ (d) ƧꓕꓤⱯIИ

94. NIRMALA
(a) ИIꓤMⱯꓶⱯ (b) ⱯꓶⱯMꓤIN
(c) AꓶAMЯIИ (d) ALAMЯIИ

95. VINAYAKA
(a) INVAYAKA (b) AKAYANIV
(c) ꓥIИⱯ⅄ⱯKⱯ (d) NIVYAAKA

96. OBSTINATE
(a) OBƧꓕIИⱯꓕE (b) BOSTINATE
(c) ETANITSBO (d) SOBTNIATE

97. PROCRASTINATE
(a) ETANITSARCORP
(b) ꓒꓤOCꓤⱯƧꓕIИⱯꓕE
(c) RPORCASTNITAE
(d) ETPROCRASTINA

98. PRECARIOUS
(a) ꓒꓤECⱯꓤIOՈƧ (b) SUOIRACERP
(c) SUOPRECARI (d) SPRECARIOU

99. PERFECTION
(a) NOITCEFERP (b) RPEFECTION
(c) ꓒEꓤꓞECꓕIOИ (d) ERPFECTION

100. FANTASY
(a) ꓞⱯИꓕⱯƧ⅄ (b) FNTSAY
(c) YSATNAF (d) YFANTSAY

☺☺☺

Darken Your Choice with HB Pencil

No.					No.					No.					No.					No.				
1.	ⓐ	ⓑ	ⓒ	ⓓ	21.	ⓐ	ⓑ	ⓒ	ⓓ	41.	ⓐ	ⓑ	ⓒ	ⓓ	61.	ⓐ	ⓑ	ⓒ	ⓓ	81.	ⓐ	ⓑ	ⓒ	ⓓ
2.	ⓐ	ⓑ	ⓒ	ⓓ	22.	ⓐ	ⓑ	ⓒ	ⓓ	42.	ⓐ	ⓑ	ⓒ	ⓓ	62.	ⓐ	ⓑ	ⓒ	ⓓ	82.	ⓐ	ⓑ	ⓒ	ⓓ
3.	ⓐ	ⓑ	ⓒ	ⓓ	23.	ⓐ	ⓑ	ⓒ	ⓓ	43.	ⓐ	ⓑ	ⓒ	ⓓ	63.	ⓐ	ⓑ	ⓒ	ⓓ	83.	ⓐ	ⓑ	ⓒ	ⓓ
4.	ⓐ	ⓑ	ⓒ	ⓓ	24.	ⓐ	ⓑ	ⓒ	ⓓ	44.	ⓐ	ⓑ	ⓒ	ⓓ	64.	ⓐ	ⓑ	ⓒ	ⓓ	84.	ⓐ	ⓑ	ⓒ	ⓓ
5.	ⓐ	ⓑ	ⓒ	ⓓ	25.	ⓐ	ⓑ	ⓒ	ⓓ	45.	ⓐ	ⓑ	ⓒ	ⓓ	65.	ⓐ	ⓑ	ⓒ	ⓓ	85.	ⓐ	ⓑ	ⓒ	ⓓ
6.	ⓐ	ⓑ	ⓒ	ⓓ	26.	ⓐ	ⓑ	ⓒ	ⓓ	46.	ⓐ	ⓑ	ⓒ	ⓓ	66.	ⓐ	ⓑ	ⓒ	ⓓ	86.	ⓐ	ⓑ	ⓒ	ⓓ
7.	ⓐ	ⓑ	ⓒ	ⓓ	27.	ⓐ	ⓑ	ⓒ	ⓓ	47.	ⓐ	ⓑ	ⓒ	ⓓ	67.	ⓐ	ⓑ	ⓒ	ⓓ	87.	ⓐ	ⓑ	ⓒ	ⓓ
8.	ⓐ	ⓑ	ⓒ	ⓓ	28.	ⓐ	ⓑ	ⓒ	ⓓ	48.	ⓐ	ⓑ	ⓒ	ⓓ	68.	ⓐ	ⓑ	ⓒ	ⓓ	88.	ⓐ	ⓑ	ⓒ	ⓓ
9.	ⓐ	ⓑ	ⓒ	ⓓ	29.	ⓐ	ⓑ	ⓒ	ⓓ	49.	ⓐ	ⓑ	ⓒ	ⓓ	69.	ⓐ	ⓑ	ⓒ	ⓓ	89.	ⓐ	ⓑ	ⓒ	ⓓ
10.	ⓐ	ⓑ	ⓒ	ⓓ	30.	ⓐ	ⓑ	ⓒ	ⓓ	50.	ⓐ	ⓑ	ⓒ	ⓓ	70.	ⓐ	ⓑ	ⓒ	ⓓ	90.	ⓐ	ⓑ	ⓒ	ⓓ
11.	ⓐ	ⓑ	ⓒ	ⓓ	31.	ⓐ	ⓑ	ⓒ	ⓓ	51.	ⓐ	ⓑ	ⓒ	ⓓ	71.	ⓐ	ⓑ	ⓒ	ⓓ	91.	ⓐ	ⓑ	ⓒ	ⓓ
12.	ⓐ	ⓑ	ⓒ	ⓓ	32.	ⓐ	ⓑ	ⓒ	ⓓ	52.	ⓐ	ⓑ	ⓒ	ⓓ	72.	ⓐ	ⓑ	ⓒ	ⓓ	92.	ⓐ	ⓑ	ⓒ	ⓓ
13.	ⓐ	ⓑ	ⓒ	ⓓ	33.	ⓐ	ⓑ	ⓒ	ⓓ	53.	ⓐ	ⓑ	ⓒ	ⓓ	73.	ⓐ	ⓑ	ⓒ	ⓓ	93.	ⓐ	ⓑ	ⓒ	ⓓ
14.	ⓐ	ⓑ	ⓒ	ⓓ	34.	ⓐ	ⓑ	ⓒ	ⓓ	54.	ⓐ	ⓑ	ⓒ	ⓓ	74.	ⓐ	ⓑ	ⓒ	ⓓ	94.	ⓐ	ⓑ	ⓒ	ⓓ
15.	ⓐ	ⓑ	ⓒ	ⓓ	35.	ⓐ	ⓑ	ⓒ	ⓓ	55.	ⓐ	ⓑ	ⓒ	ⓓ	75.	ⓐ	ⓑ	ⓒ	ⓓ	95.	ⓐ	ⓑ	ⓒ	ⓓ
16.	ⓐ	ⓑ	ⓒ	ⓓ	36.	ⓐ	ⓑ	ⓒ	ⓓ	56.	ⓐ	ⓑ	ⓒ	ⓓ	76.	ⓐ	ⓑ	ⓒ	ⓓ	96.	ⓐ	ⓑ	ⓒ	ⓓ
17.	ⓐ	ⓑ	ⓒ	ⓓ	37.	ⓐ	ⓑ	ⓒ	ⓓ	57.	ⓐ	ⓑ	ⓒ	ⓓ	77.	ⓐ	ⓑ	ⓒ	ⓓ	97.	ⓐ	ⓑ	ⓒ	ⓓ
18.	ⓐ	ⓑ	ⓒ	ⓓ	38.	ⓐ	ⓑ	ⓒ	ⓓ	58.	ⓐ	ⓑ	ⓒ	ⓓ	78.	ⓐ	ⓑ	ⓒ	ⓓ	98.	ⓐ	ⓑ	ⓒ	ⓓ
19.	ⓐ	ⓑ	ⓒ	ⓓ	39.	ⓐ	ⓑ	ⓒ	ⓓ	59.	ⓐ	ⓑ	ⓒ	ⓓ	79.	ⓐ	ⓑ	ⓒ	ⓓ	99.	ⓐ	ⓑ	ⓒ	ⓓ
20.	ⓐ	ⓑ	ⓒ	ⓓ	40.	ⓐ	ⓑ	ⓒ	ⓓ	60.	ⓐ	ⓑ	ⓒ	ⓓ	80.	ⓐ	ⓑ	ⓒ	ⓓ	100.	ⓐ	ⓑ	ⓒ	ⓓ

WORKBOOK

Achievers Section

Multiple Choice Questions

1. If one third of a tank holds 60 litres of water, then the quantity of water that half tank holds is ________.
   (a) 60 litres (b) 80 litres
   (c) 90 litres (d) 120 litres

2. What fraction of an hour is a second?
   (a) $\frac{1}{60}$ (b) $\frac{1}{120}$
   (c) $\frac{1}{360}$ (d) $\frac{1}{3600}$

3. $\frac{3}{8}$ is what part of $\frac{1}{12}$?
   (a) $\frac{7}{2}$ (b) $\frac{9}{2}$
   (c) $\frac{2}{9}$ (d) $\frac{4}{3}$

4. Which of the following fractions is the smallest?
   (a) $\frac{7}{8}$ (b) $\frac{17}{21}$
   (c) $\frac{13}{16}$ (d) $\frac{15}{19}$

5. $2 + 0.2 + 0.02 + 0.002 = ?$
   (a) 2.232 (b) 2.032
   (c) 2.022 (d) 2.222

6. In the following figure, what is the measure of ∠AOB?

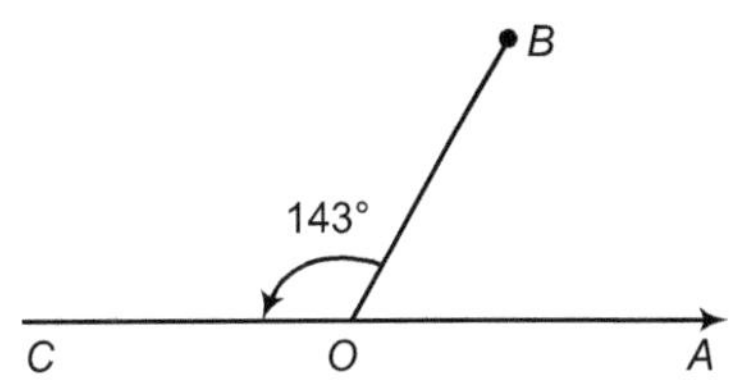

   (a) 37° (b) 27°
   (c) 47° (d) 57°

7. What is the complementary angle of 67°?
   (a) 13° (b) 23°
   (c) 33° (d) 43°

8. Which of the following cannot be sides of a triangle?
   (a) 3 cm, 4 cm, 5 cm
   (b) 4 cm, 6 cm, 10 cm
   (c) 6 cm, 7 cm, 9 cm
   (d) 5 cm, 12 cm, 13 cm

9. Which of the following is a prime number?
   (a) 61 (b) 63
   (c) 49 (d) 87

10. Which of the following is not a prime number?
    (a) 97 (b) 67
    (c) 69 (d) 43

11. How many days are there in a leap year?
    (a) 365 days (b) 366 days
    (c) 367 days (d) None of these

12. How many hours are there in February 2004?
    (a) 1440 (b) 1540
    (c) 1640 (d) 696

13. What is the sum of 7 kg 50 gm, 9 kg 970 gm and 12 kg 335 gm?
(a) 29 kg 335 gm (b) 28 kg 765 gm
(c) 29 kg 345 gm (d) 29 kg 355 gm

14. What is the difference between 7 litres 15 ml and 5 litres 870 ml?
(a) 2 litre 145 ml (b) 1 litre 145 ml
(c) 1 litre 165 ml (d) 1 litre 155 ml

15. How many seconds are there in 2 hours 15 minutes?
(a) 7260 seconds (b) 8100 seconds
(c) 7800 seconds (d) None of these

16. How many millimeters are there in 7 metres and 17 centimetres?
(a) 7170 mm (b) 7107 mm
(c) 7017 mm (d) None of these

17. How many feet are there in 192 inches?
(a) 14 (b) 15
(c) 16 (d) 17

18. Ram has a ₹ 2000 note. He bought some books which cost ₹ 795, some notebooks which cost ₹ 435 and some pens for ₹ 295. How much money is left with Ram?
(a) ₹ 455 (b) ₹ 495
(c) ₹ 465 (d) ₹ 475

19. Evaluate $65 - 75 \div 15 + (14 - 6) + 27$?
(a) 75 (b) 85
(c) 95 (d) 105

20. Evaluate $137 - (17 + 23) + 150 \div 25 - 18$?
(a) 65 (b) 75
(c) 85 (d) 95

21. What is the difference between the largest three digit number and smallest four digit number?
(a) 1 (b) 0
(c) 101 (d) 1999

22. What is the sum of largest four digit number and largest three digit number?
(a) 11998 (b) 10999
(c) 9998 (d) 10998

23. How many days are there if the days of January, March and June of any year is added?
(a) 91 days (b) 92 days
(c) 93 days (d) None of these

24. Evaluate $\frac{1}{8}+\frac{1}{7}+\frac{1}{9}$
(a) $\frac{171}{504}$ (b) $\frac{191}{504}$
(c) $\frac{181}{504}$ (d) None of these

25. Which of the following is not a proper fraction?
(a) $\frac{7}{9}$ (b) $\frac{7}{13}$
(c) $\frac{5}{12}$ (d) $\frac{7}{5}$

26. Which of the following fractions is the largest?
(a) $\frac{2}{7}$ (b) $\frac{3}{11}$
(c) $\frac{7}{12}$ (d) $\frac{8}{17}$

27. Which of the given decimal number is the largest, 2.392, 2.089, 2.907, 2.968, 2.579, 2.98.
(a) 2.98 (b) 2.968
(c) 2.907 (d) 2.579

28. Five bells commence tolling together and toll at intervals of 6, 7, 8, 9 and 12 seconds. After how many seconds they will toll together?
(a) 504 seconds (b) 512 seconds
(c) 612 seconds (d) None of these

29. Which of the following is the largest number which can divide 105, 1001 and 2436?
(a) 3 (b) 7
(c) 11 (d) 21

30. Find the largest number which when divides 1050, 1250 and 1650 leaves remainder 43, 31 and 7 respectively.
(a) 53 (b) 57
(c) 59 (d) 73

31. H.C.F. of two numbers is 11 and their L.C.M. is 693. If one of the numbers is 99. What is the other number?
(a) 66 (b) 77
(c) 88 (d) None of these

32. What is the L.C.M. of $\frac{4}{5}, \frac{5}{6}$ and $\frac{6}{7}$?
(a) 90 (b) 120
(c) 140 (d) 150

33. What is the sum of the largest four digit number and the smallest four digit number formed by the digit 2, 3, 8, 7 if digits are not repeated?
(a) 12110 (b) 11010
(c) 10110 (d) 11110

34. What is the difference between the largest four digit number and the smallest four digit number made by the digits, 7, 6, 0, 4, if repetition of digits is not allowed?
(a) 3473 (b) 3573
(c) 3583 (d) None of these

35. Which of the following is a reflex angle?
(a) 167° (b) 193°
(c) 99° (d) 360°

36. Which of the following numbers should come in place of * to make the number divisible by 3?
7426*58
(a) 0 (b) 1
(c) 2 (d) 3

37. What is the value of $631 + 1200 \div 6 \times 2 + 417 \times 2$?
(a) 1765 (b) 1835
(c) 1845 (d) 1865

38. What is the value of $624.7 - 378.943$?
(a) 245.757 (b) 237.757
(c) 257.757 (d) 247.557

39. The angles of a triangle are in the ratio 2 : 5 : 8. What is the measure of the largest angle?
(a) 72° (b) 60°
(c) 84° (d) 96°

40. The sides of a triangle are 7 cm, 17 cm, 25 cm. What is its perimeter?
(a) 46 cm (b) 47 cm
(c) 48 cm (d) 49 cm

41. What is the area and circumference of a circle if its radius is 7 cm?
(a) 154 cm^2, 44 cm
(b) 154 cm^2, 77 cm
(c) 154 cm^2, 34 cm
(d) None of these

42. Which of the following expressions is true?
(a) $3.075 < 3.069$
(b) $3.73 > 3.597$
(c) $3.029 > 3.198$
(d) $3.602 > 3.7$

43. In a box there are 57032 black balls, 90736 red balls and 67693 green balls. What is the total number of balls?
(a) 215461 (b) 217461
(c) 215451 (d) 215471

44. Find the smallest number which when divided by 12, 15, 20 or 54 leaves a remainder 6 in each case?
(a) 546 (b) 446
(c) 556 (d) 456

45. If A : B = 3 : 5, B : C = 2 : 3 What is the value of A : B : C?
(a) 2 : 3 : 5 (b) 6 : 10 : 15
(c) 15 : 10 : 6 (d) 10 : 6 : 15

46. What is the Roman numeral of 524?
(a) DXIV (b) DXXIV
(c) MXXIV (d) None of these

47. Roman numeral XCIX is equivalent to ______.
(a) 99 (b) 109
(c) 98 (d) None of these

48. What will be the dividend if remainder is 17, divisor is 157 and quotient is 308?
(a) 47,373 (b) 48,353
(c) 48,373 (d) 49,373

49. If the diagonal of a square is $8\sqrt{2}$ cm, then what is its perimeter?
   (a) 32 cm (b) 48 cm
   (c) 64 cm (d) 72 cm

50. How many right angles may be possible in a triangle?
   (a) 1 (b) 2
   (c) 3 (d) None of these

Darken Your Choice with HB Pencil

1.	ⓐ ⓑ ⓒ ⓓ	11.	ⓐ ⓑ ⓒ ⓓ	21.	ⓐ ⓑ ⓒ ⓓ	31.	ⓐ ⓑ ⓒ ⓓ	41.	ⓐ ⓑ ⓒ ⓓ
2.	ⓐ ⓑ ⓒ ⓓ	12.	ⓐ ⓑ ⓒ ⓓ	22.	ⓐ ⓑ ⓒ ⓓ	32.	ⓐ ⓑ ⓒ ⓓ	42.	ⓐ ⓑ ⓒ ⓓ
3.	ⓐ ⓑ ⓒ ⓓ	13.	ⓐ ⓑ ⓒ ⓓ	23.	ⓐ ⓑ ⓒ ⓓ	33.	ⓐ ⓑ ⓒ ⓓ	43.	ⓐ ⓑ ⓒ ⓓ
4.	ⓐ ⓑ ⓒ ⓓ	14.	ⓐ ⓑ ⓒ ⓓ	24.	ⓐ ⓑ ⓒ ⓓ	34.	ⓐ ⓑ ⓒ ⓓ	44.	ⓐ ⓑ ⓒ ⓓ
5.	ⓐ ⓑ ⓒ ⓓ	15.	ⓐ ⓑ ⓒ ⓓ	25.	ⓐ ⓑ ⓒ ⓓ	35.	ⓐ ⓑ ⓒ ⓓ	45.	ⓐ ⓑ ⓒ ⓓ
6.	ⓐ ⓑ ⓒ ⓓ	16.	ⓐ ⓑ ⓒ ⓓ	26.	ⓐ ⓑ ⓒ ⓓ	36.	ⓐ ⓑ ⓒ ⓓ	46.	ⓐ ⓑ ⓒ ⓓ
7.	ⓐ ⓑ ⓒ ⓓ	17.	ⓐ ⓑ ⓒ ⓓ	27.	ⓐ ⓑ ⓒ ⓓ	37.	ⓐ ⓑ ⓒ ⓓ	47.	ⓐ ⓑ ⓒ ⓓ
8.	ⓐ ⓑ ⓒ ⓓ	18.	ⓐ ⓑ ⓒ ⓓ	28.	ⓐ ⓑ ⓒ ⓓ	38.	ⓐ ⓑ ⓒ ⓓ	48.	ⓐ ⓑ ⓒ ⓓ
9.	ⓐ ⓑ ⓒ ⓓ	19.	ⓐ ⓑ ⓒ ⓓ	29.	ⓐ ⓑ ⓒ ⓓ	39.	ⓐ ⓑ ⓒ ⓓ	49.	ⓐ ⓑ ⓒ ⓓ
10.	ⓐ ⓑ ⓒ ⓓ	20.	ⓐ ⓑ ⓒ ⓓ	30.	ⓐ ⓑ ⓒ ⓓ	40.	ⓐ ⓑ ⓒ ⓓ	50.	ⓐ ⓑ ⓒ ⓓ

WORKBOOK

Hints and Solutions

1. NUMBER SENSE

Answer Key

1. (b)	2. (d)	3. (a)	4. (a)	5. (a)	6. (a)	7. (b)	8. (b)	9. (b)	10. (c)
11. (d)	12. (a)	13. (d)	14. (d)	15. (c)	16. (b)	17. (a)	18. (c)	19. (a)	20. (a)
21. (b)	22. (b)	23. (c)	24. (d)	25. (b)	26. (c)	27. (a)	28. (a)	29. (c)	30. (c)
31. (a)	32. (d)	33. (b)	34. (c)	35. (a)	36. (d)	37. (b)	38. (a)	39. (a)	40. (a)
41. (a)	42. (b)	43. (a)	44. (a)	45. (b)	46. (a)	47. (a)	48. (a)	49. (b)	50. (c)

23. Prime numbers between 50 and 70 are

53, 59, 61, 67

Sum = 53 + 59 + 61 + 67 = 240

24. Prime numbers between 1 and 30 are

2, 3, 5, 7, 11, 13, 17, 19, 23, 29

Sum = 2 + 3 + 5 + 7 + 11 + 13 + 17 + 19 + 23 + 29 = 129

35. Difference = 8760 – 6078

= 2682

2. OPERATIONS ON NUMBERS

Answer Key

1. (b)	2. (c)	3. (b)	4. (b)	5. (c)	6. (a)	7. (b)	8. (d)	9. (b)	10. (a)
11. (c)	12. (d)	13. (c)	14. (d)	15. (d)	16. (a)	17. (a)	18. (a)	19. (b)	20. (d)
21. (b)	22. (c)	23. (a)	24. (a)	25. (d)	26. (d)	27. (c)	28. (b)	29. (d)	30. (a)
31. (c)	32. (d)	33. (b)	34. (d)	35. (a)	36. (c)	37. (b)	38. (b)	39. (b)	40. (b)
41. (c)	42. (a)	43. (c)	44. (c)	45. (c)	46. (c)	47. (b)	48. (b)	49. (a)	50. (a)

4. Largest five digit number = 99999

   Smallest five digit number = 10000

   Difference = 99999 – 10000 = 89999

6. Number of female members

   = 503709 – 279447

   = 224262

8. Number of boxes $= \frac{2540160}{144} = 17640$

9. Number of tiles = 36 × 4 × 172 = 24768

14. $\frac{547}{18} = 30\frac{7}{18}$

    Remainder = 7

22. $(3 + 4)^2 - 5 \times 3 + 3^2$

    $= 7^2 - 15 + 9$

    $= 49 + 9 - 15 = 43$

23. $(27 \div 3 + 4) - (2^3 - 2 \times 7)$

    $= (9 + 4) - (8 - 14)$

    $= 13 + 6$

    $= 19$

24. $(4^3 \div 8 + 7) - (3^2 - 7 \times 2)$

    $= (64 \div 8 + 7) - (9 - 14)$

    $= (8 + 7) - (-5)$

    $= 15 + 5$

    $= 20$

25. $(7^3 - 2 \times 13) + (5 \times 7 - 2^3)$

    $= (343 - 26) + (35 - 8)$

    $= 317 + 27$

    $= 344$

26. $5 + 7 \times 2 - 32 \div 4$

    $= 5 + 7 \times 2 - 8$

    $= 5 + 14 - 8$

    $= 19 - 8$

    $= 11$

27. $71 - 24 - 75 \div 15 + 17$

    $= 71 - 24 - 5 + 17$

    $= 88 - 29$

    $= 59$

28. $4^3 + 19 \times 3 - 67$

    $= 64 + 57 - 67$

    $= 64 - 10$

    $= 54$

29. $17 \times 2 + 7 - 175 \div 7$

    $= 17 \times 2 + 7 - 25$

    $= 34 + 7 - 25$

    $= 41 - 25$

    $= 16$

30. $52 - 4^3 + (8 \times 17) \div 4$

    $= 52 - 64 + 136 \div 4$

    $= 52 - 64 + 34$

    $= 52 - 30$

    $= 22$

37.
$$\begin{array}{r} 10000000 \\ -\ \ 6705097 \\ \hline 3294903 \\ \hline \end{array}$$

39.
$$\begin{array}{r} 765938 \\ +\ 460353 \\ \hline 1226291 \\ \hline \end{array}$$

$$\begin{array}{r} 1226291 \\ -\ \ 892097 \\ \hline 334194 \\ \hline \end{array}$$

3. DECIMALS AND FRACTIONS

Answer Key

1. (d)	2. (d)	3. (b)	4. (c)	5. (d)	6. (b)	7. (a)	8. (b)	9. (c)	10. (b)
11. (a)	12. (c)	13. (c)	14. (b)	15. (a)	16. (a)	17. (a)	18. (b)	19. (b)	20. (c)
21. (d)	22. (d)	23. (a)	24. (c)	25. (b)	26. (b)	27. (a)	28. (c)	29. (a)	30. (a)
31. (a)	32. (d)	33. (a)	34. (c)	35. (d)	36. (b)	37. (a)	38. (b)	39. (b)	40. (a)
41. (a)	42. (d)	43. (d)	44. (d)	45. (a)	46. (b)	47. (b)	48. (d)	49. (b)	50. (c)
51. (c)	52. (b)	53. (c)	54. (c)	55. (b)	56. (d)	57. (a)	58. (a)	59. (b)	60. (b)

2. $\frac{4}{5} = 0.8, \frac{3}{7} = 0.42, \frac{5}{6} = 0.83, \frac{2}{7} = 0.28$

$\frac{5}{6} > \frac{4}{5} > \frac{3}{7} > \frac{2}{7}$

3. $\frac{5}{8} = 0.62, \frac{6}{7} = 0.85, \frac{7}{9} = 0.77, \frac{8}{11} = 0.72$

$\frac{6}{7} > \frac{7}{9} > \frac{8}{11} > \frac{5}{8}$

18. $5.6401 - 5.0629 = 0.5772$

19. $\frac{1}{4}$ of $x = 28$

$x = 28 \times 4 = 112$

$\frac{1}{2}$ of $112 = \frac{112}{2} = 56$

45. $\frac{7}{9} = 0.77, \frac{2}{3} = 0.66, \frac{5}{8} = 0.62, \frac{7}{11} = 0.63$

$\frac{7}{9} > \frac{2}{3} > \frac{7}{11} > \frac{5}{8}$

46. $\frac{11}{13} = 0.84, \frac{13}{17} = 0.76, \frac{7}{9} = 0.77$

$\frac{17}{19} = 0.89$

$\frac{17}{19} > \frac{11}{13} > \frac{7}{9} > \frac{13}{17}$

51. $7.007 + 7.067 + 7.027 = 21.101$

52. $12.863 - 12.002 = 0.861$

53. $\frac{2}{7} = 0.285, \frac{3}{5} = 0.6, \frac{1}{8} = 0.125, \frac{7}{9} = 0.777$

$\frac{1}{8} < \frac{2}{7} < \frac{3}{5} < \frac{7}{9}$

54. $\frac{2}{13} = 0.153, \frac{3}{17} = 0.176, \frac{7}{15} = 0.466$

$\frac{8}{19} = 0.421$

$\frac{2}{13} < \frac{3}{17} < \frac{8}{19} < \frac{7}{15}$

Largest fraction $= \frac{7}{15}$

55. $4.003 \times 7.03 = 28.141$

56. $1.029 < 1.079 < 1.097 < 1.109$

Largest $= 1.109$

57. $2.003 < 2.007 < 2.103 < 2.907$

Smallest $= 2.003$

58. $3.007 \times 7.027 = 21.13$

59. $100 - 79.997 = 20.003$

60. $5.007 < 5.072 < 5.707 < 5.777$

4. LEAST COMMON MULTIPLE AND HIGHEST COMMON FACTOR

Answer Key

1. (a)	2. (c)	3. (a)	4. (c)	5. (a)	6. (c)	7. (c)	8. (b)	9. (c)	10. (b)
11. (b)	12. (a)	13. (c)	14. (a)	15. (b)	16. (c)	17. (b)	18. (c)	19. (b)	20. (c)
21. (b)	22. (a)	23. (c)	24. (a)	25. (c)	26. (b)	27. (c)	28. (c)	29. (b)	30. (a)
31. (c)	32. (b)	33. (a)	34. (b)	35. (c)	36. (c)	37. (c)	38. (c)	39. (b)	40. (c)
41. (c)	42. (a)	43. (a)	44. (c)	45. (b)	46. (c)	47. (c)	48. (d)	49. (b)	50. (c)

3. H.C.F. of (91 – 43), (183 – 91) and (183 – 43)

H.C.F. of 48, 92, 140 = 4

4.

3	7, 15, 18, 27
3	7, 5, 6, 9
	7, 5, 2, 3

L.C.M. = 2 × 3 × 3 × 3 ×5 × 7

= 54 × 35 = 1890

14.

3	6, 18, 27, 39
3	2, 6, 9, 13
2	2, 2, 3, 13
	1, 1, 3, 13

L.C.M. = 2 × 3 × 3 × 3 × 13 = 54 × 13 = 702

33.

2	4, 6, 7, 9
3	2, 3, 7, 9
	2, 1, 7, 3

L.C.M. = 2 × 2 × 3 × 3 × 7 = 12 × 21 = 252

36.

2	8, 9, 12, 16, 21
2	4, 9, 6, 8, 21
2	2, 9, 3, 4, 21
3	1, 9, 3, 2, 21
	1, 3, 1, 2, 7

L.C.M. = 2 × 2 × 2 × 2 × 3 × 3 ×7

= 48 × 21

= 1008

37.

2	16, 24, 30, 45, 50
2	8, 12, 15, 45, 25
2	4, 6, 15, 45, 25
3	2, 3, 15, 45, 25
5	2, 1, 5, 15, 25
	2, 1, 1, 3, 5

L.C.M. = 2 × 2 × 2 × 2 × 3 × 3 × 5 × 5

= 48 × 75 = 3600

39. H.C.F. of 385, 700 and 1295 = 35

42. H.C.F. of two numbers = 37

Let the numbers be $37x$ and $37y$

$$37x \times 37y = 4107$$

$$xy = \frac{4107}{37 \times 37} = 3$$

$$x = 1 \text{ or } y = 3$$

The numbers are 37 × 1 = 37 and

37 × 3 = 111

Difference = 111 – 37 = 74

49. L.C.M. of 12, 16, 18, 21, 28 + 7

= 1008 + 7 = 1015

5. MEASUREMENT AND TEMPERATURE

Answer Key

1. (d)	2. (a)	3. (b)	4. (b)	5. (b)	6. (d)	7. (b)	8. (c)	9. (a)	10. (a)
11. (c)	12. (c)	13. (a)	14. (a)	15.(b)	16. (b)	17. (a)	18. (a)	19. (b)	20. (d)
21. (d)	22. (b)	23. (b)	24. (d)	25. (b)	26. (b)	27. (b)	28. (a)	29. (b)	30. (c)
31. (d)	32. (c)	33. (a)	34. (b)	35. (d)	36. (d)	37. (a)	38. (b)	39. (c)	40. (d)
41. (a)	42. (a)	43. (d)	44. (a)	45. (c)	46. (a)	47. (a)	48. (a)	49. (c)	50. (c)

3.
$$\begin{array}{rrr} & \text{Feet} & \text{Inch} \\ & 4 & 7 \\ - & 3 & 11 \\ \hline \end{array}$$

$$\begin{array}{rrr} & \text{Feet} & \text{Inch} \\ & 3 & 19 \\ - & 3 & 11 \\ \hline & & 8 \\ \hline \end{array}$$

$\Rightarrow$

4.
$$\begin{array}{rrr} & \text{Km} & \text{m} \\ & 8 & 300 \\ - & 6 & 800 \\ \hline \end{array}$$

$$\Rightarrow \begin{array}{rrr} & \text{Km} & \text{m} \\ & 7 & 1300 \\ - & 6 & 800 \\ \hline & 1 & 500 \\ \hline \end{array}$$

5.
$$\begin{array}{rrr} & \text{m} & \text{cm} \\ & 9 & 15 \\ - & 7 & 85 \\ \hline \end{array}$$

$$\Rightarrow \begin{array}{rrr} & \text{m} & \text{cm} \\ & 8 & 115 \\ - & 7 & 85 \\ \hline & 1 & 30 \\ \hline \end{array}$$

6.
$$\begin{array}{rrr} & \text{kg} & \text{gm} \\ & 15 & 250 \\ - & 12 & 850 \\ \hline \end{array} \Rightarrow \begin{array}{rrr} & \text{kg} & \text{gm} \\ & 14 & 1250 \\ - & 12 & 850 \\ \hline & 2 & 400 \\ \hline \end{array}$$

8.
$$\begin{array}{rrr} & \text{Feet} & \text{inch} \\ & 8 & 2 \\ - & 6 & 8 \\ \hline \end{array} \Rightarrow \begin{array}{rrr} & \text{Feet} & \text{inch} \\ & 7 & 14 \\ - & 6 & 8 \\ \hline & 1 & 6 \\ \hline \end{array}$$

9. 7 m 40 cm = 7 × 100 + 40 = 740 cm

10. 8000 m $= \frac{8000}{1000} = 8$ km

11. $\frac{140000}{1000} = 140$ tonnes

12. $\frac{2860}{1000} = 2.86\,l$

13. $\frac{73450}{1000} = 73.450$ kg

18. $\frac{76}{12} = 6.33$ feet

19.
$$\begin{array}{rrr} & \text{litre} & \text{millilitre} \\ & 50 & 000 \\ - & 43 & 200 \\ \hline \end{array} \Rightarrow \begin{array}{rrr} & \text{litre} & \text{millilitre} \\ & 49 & 1000 \\ - & 43 & 200 \\ \hline & 6 & 800 \\ \hline \end{array}$$

24.
$$\begin{array}{rrr} & \text{litre} & \text{millilitre} \\ & 16 & 450 \\ + & 17 & 695 \\ \hline & 34 & 145 \\ \hline \end{array}$$

25.

	litre	millilitre
	39	650
+	43	550
	83	200

30. 12 minutes = 12 × 60 = 720 seconds

31. 25 days = 25 × 24 = 600 hours

32. 1 day = 24 hours = 24 × 60

= 1440 minutes

35. 2 km = 2 × 1000 = 2000 m

= 2000 × 100 = 200000 cm

36. 12 feet = 12 × 12 = 144 inches

37. $\frac{C}{5} = \frac{F-32}{9}$

$\frac{C}{5} = \frac{41-32}{9}$

$\Rightarrow \frac{C}{5} = 1$

$\Rightarrow C = 5$

38. $\frac{C}{5} = \frac{F-32}{9}$

$\frac{20}{5} = \frac{F-32}{9} \Rightarrow 36 = F - 32$

$F = 36 + 32 = 68°$

39. $\frac{C}{5} = \frac{F-32}{9}$

$\frac{25}{5} = \frac{F-32}{9}$

$\Rightarrow F - 32 = 45$

$F = 32 + 45 = 77$

40. $\frac{C}{5} = \frac{F-32}{9}$

$\Rightarrow \frac{C}{5} = \frac{18-32}{9}$

$C = \frac{5 \times (-14)}{9} = -7.7°$

41. $\frac{C}{5} = \frac{F-32}{9} \Rightarrow \frac{C}{5} = \frac{101.3-32}{9}$

$C = \frac{5 \times 69.3}{9} = 38.5°$

42. $\frac{C}{5} = \frac{F-32}{9} \Rightarrow \frac{100}{5} = \frac{F-32}{9}$

$F - 32 = 180$

$\Rightarrow F = 180 + 32 = 212°$

43. $\frac{C}{5} = \frac{F-32}{9}$

$\Rightarrow \frac{57}{5} = \frac{F-32}{9}$

$F = 11.4 \times 9 + 32 = 134.6°$

44. $\frac{C}{5} = \frac{F-32}{9}$

$\frac{C}{5} = \frac{90-32}{9}$

$C = \frac{58}{9} \times 5 = 6.44 \times 5 = 32.2°C$

45. $\frac{C}{5} = \frac{F-32}{9}$

$\frac{C}{5} = \frac{106-32}{9}$

$C = 5 \times \frac{74}{9} = 5 \times 8.22 = 41.1°$

46. $\frac{C}{5} = \frac{F-32}{9}$

$\frac{40}{5} = \frac{F-32}{9}$

$F = 9 \times 8 + 32 = 72 + 32 = 104°$

6. MONEY

Answer Key

1. (b)	2. (c)	3. (d)	4. (a)	5. (c)	6. (d)	7. (b)	8. (b)	9. (d)	10. (d)
11. (c)	12. (d)	13. (c)	14. (a)	15. (b)	16. (c)	17. (b)	18. (b)	19. (a)	20. (d)
21. (b)	22. (c)	23. (c)	24. (b)	25. (d)	26. (a)	27. (b)	28. (a)	29. (b)	30. (c)

1. 5000 – (575 + 1340 + 1739)
   = 5000 – 3654 = ₹ 1346
2. 2 × 10 + 4 × 20 + 2 × 100 + 1 × 500
   = 20 + 80 + 200 + 500
   = ₹ 800
   Balance = 800 – 785 = ₹ 15
3. Total expenses = 3600 + 2400 + 125
   = ₹ 6125
4. Total expenses = 580 + 8 × 45 + 6 × 16
   = 580 + 360 + 96
   = ₹ 1036
   Money left with Mohit = 2000 – 1036 = ₹ 964
5. Cost of 1 litre petrol = ₹ 71.75
   Cost of 4 litres petrol = 71.75 × 4 = ₹ 287
6. Total expenses during journey
   = 1440 + 380 + 220
   = ₹ 2,040
7. Cost of 2 dozen eggs = 2 × 20 = ₹ 40
   Required money = 100 – 40 = ₹ 60
8. Required money = 2000 – 530 = ₹ 1470
9. 12 apples weigh 1 kg
   Cost of 1 kg apple = ₹ 30
10. Cost of 1 kg oranges = 2 × 23 = ₹ 46
12. Total amount = 3 × 500 + 4 × 100 + 3 × 50
    = 1500 + 400 + 150 = ₹ 2050
13. Total expenses = 2400 + 1500 + 2600 + 2300
    = ₹ 8800
    Savings = 14600 – 8800 = ₹ 5800
14. Cost of sweets = 25 × 12 = ₹ 300
    Required amount = 500 – 300 = ₹ 200
15. Total amount = 2 × 2000 + 1 × 500 + 1 × 100
    = 4000 + 500 + 100 = ₹ 4600
16. Total bill = 2 × 130 + 6 × 18 + 2 × 56
    = 260 + 108 + 112
    = ₹ 480
17. Total amount = 2 × 500 + 7 × 100 + 6 × 50 + 5 × 20
    = 1000 + 700 + 300 + 100
    = ₹ 2100
18. Earning in 30 days = $\frac{230}{10} \times 30 = 690$
21. Cost of fencing per metre = $\frac{300}{5 \times 4}$ = ₹15
23. 770 +320 = ₹ 1090
28. Expenses = 760 + 340 + 15 × 40
    = 760 + 340 + 600 = ₹ 1700
    Money left with Mohit = 2000 – 1700 = ₹ 300
29. $\frac{1000}{250} = 4$ kg
30. Total cost = 875 + 435 + 175 = 1485

7. RATIO AND PROPORTION

Answer Key

1. (b)	2. (b)	3. (b)	4. (d)	5. (b)	6. (c)	7. (c)	8. (b)	9. (a)	10. (a)
11. (d)	12. (b)	13. (b)	14. (d)	15. (b)	16. (d)	17. (b)	18. (b)	19. (c)	20. (d)
21. (a)	22. (a)	23. (b)	24. (c)	25. (b)	26. (c)	27. (d)	28. (c)	29. (b)	30. (b)
31. (d)	32. (b)	33. (c)	34. (c)	35. (c)	36. (a)	37. (b)	38. (d)	39. (c)	40. (c)
41. (b)	42. (a)	43. (b)	44. (d)	45. (c)	46. (c)	47. (b)	48. (c)	49. (d)	50. (d)

4. $7k + 9k = 144$

$\Rightarrow \quad k = \frac{144}{16} = 9$

Difference $= 9k - 7k = 2k = 2 \times 9 = 18$

7. Present age of Amir $= 4k$

Present age of Sonal $= 5k$,

According to question,

$$\frac{4k - 18}{5k - 18} = \frac{11}{16}$$

$64k - 288 = 55k - 198$

$64k - 55k = 288 - 198 = 90$

$9k = 90$

$\Rightarrow k = 10$

Present age of Amir $= 4 \times 10$

$= 40$ years

17. Expense $= 16400 - 9000 = 7400$

Required ratio $= \frac{7400}{9000} = \frac{37}{45} = 37 : 45$

18. $49 : P :: P : 16$

$$\frac{49}{P} = \frac{P}{16}$$

$\Rightarrow \quad P^2 = 49 \times 16$

$P = \sqrt{49 \times 16} = 7 \times 4 = 28$

19. Expenditure $= 14800 - 3200 = 11600$

Required ratio $= \frac{3200}{11600} = \frac{32}{116} = \frac{8}{29} = 8 : 29$

20. Share of Sumit $= \frac{3}{2+3+4} \times ₹\,8100$

$= \frac{3}{9} \times 8100$

$= ₹\,2700$

21. Shekhar's share $= \frac{5}{2+3+5} \times ₹\,2040$

$= \frac{5}{10} \times 2040$

$= 5 \times 204 = ₹\,1020$

36. Share of $N = \frac{40}{45+36+40} \times 12100$

$= \frac{40}{121} \times 12100 = 4000$

37. $12x = 180$

$\Rightarrow \quad x = \frac{180}{12} = 15$

Difference $= 4x - 3x = x = 15$

38. $4 : 9 :: 12 : x$

$$\frac{4}{9} = \frac{12}{x}$$

$$12 \times 9 = 4x$$
$$108 = 4x$$
$$x = \frac{108}{4} = 27$$

44. $\frac{40 \text{ cm}}{1 \text{ km}} = \frac{40 \text{ cm}}{1 \times 1000 \times 100 \text{ cm}}$

$$= \frac{4}{10000} = \frac{1}{2500} = 1:2500$$

45. $\frac{6 \text{ inches}}{3 \text{ feet}} = \frac{6 \text{ inches}}{3 \times 12 \text{ inches}} = \frac{1}{6} = 1:6$

46. Cost of 1 Pen $= \frac{65}{5} = ₹\,13$

Cost of 1 Pencil $= \frac{84}{12} = ₹\,7$

Required ratio $= \frac{7}{13} = 7:13$

8. AREA, PERIMETER AND VOLUME

Answer Key

1. (a)	2. (a)	3. (d)	4. (c)	5. (d)	6. (a)	7. (c)	8. (b)	9. (b)	10. (a)
11. (c)	12. (a)	13. (a)	14. (b)	15. (c)	16. (b)	17. (a)	18. (c)	19. (c)	20. (b)
21. (b)	22. (d)	23. (c)	24. (c)	25. (b)	26. (c)	27. (b)	28. (b)	29. (d)	30. (d)
31. (d)	32. (c)	33. (b)	34. (c)	35. (b)	36. (d)	37. (b)	38. (c)	39. (c)	40. (a)
41. (a)	42. (b)	43. (c)	44. (d)	45. (a)	46. (b)	47. (d)	48. (d)	49. (b)	50. (c)
51. (d)	52. (d)	53. (a)	54. (a)	55. (c)	56. (d)	57. (b)	58. (b)	59. (d)	60. (d)

1. Side of square $= \frac{44}{4} = 11$ cm

   Area = $(\text{side})^2 = 11^2 = 121 \text{ cm}^2$

2. Perimeter of rectangle = 42

   $2(l + b) = 42$

   $\Rightarrow \; l + b = \frac{42}{2} = 21$

   $15 + b = 21$

   $\Rightarrow \; b = 21 - 15 = 6$ cm

3. Area of rectangle

   $= l \times b = 15 \times 12 = 180 \text{ cm}^2$

4. Length of diagonal $= a\sqrt{2} = 8\sqrt{2}$ cm

5. Area of square

   $= \frac{1}{2} \times (\text{diagonal})^2 = \frac{1}{2} \times (6\sqrt{2})^2 = 36 \text{ cm}^2$

7. $2\pi r = 176$

   $2 \times \frac{22}{7} \times r = 176$

   $\Rightarrow \; r = \frac{176 \times 7}{44} = 28$

   Area $= \pi r^2 = \frac{22}{7} \times 28^2 = \frac{22}{7} \times 28 \times 28$

   $= 88 \times 28 = 2464 \text{ cm}^2$

8. Area $= \pi r^2 = \frac{22}{7} \times \left(\frac{14}{2}\right)^2 = \frac{22}{7} \times 7 \times 7$

   $= 154 \text{ cm}^2$

9. Area of triangle $= \frac{1}{2} \times \text{base} \times \text{height}$

$= \frac{1}{2} \times 10 \times 24 = 120 \text{ cm}^2$

10. Area of equilateral triangle

$= \frac{\sqrt{3}}{4} \times (\text{side})^2$

$= \frac{\sqrt{3}}{4} \times 8^2 = 16\sqrt{3} \text{ cm}^2$

11. Side $= \frac{\text{Diagonal}}{\sqrt{2}} = \frac{20}{\sqrt{2}} = \frac{10 \times 2}{\sqrt{2}} = 10\sqrt{2}$

Perimeter $= 4 \times 10\sqrt{2} = 40\sqrt{2}$ cm

12. Area = 7500

$3x \times 4x = 7500$

$\Rightarrow \quad x^2 = \frac{7500}{12} = 625$

$x = \sqrt{625} = 25$

Perimeter = 2(75 + 100) = 2 × 175 = 350 m

26. Area $= \frac{\sqrt{3}}{4} \times (\text{side})^2$

$= \frac{\sqrt{3}}{4} \times (4\sqrt{3})^2$

$= \frac{\sqrt{3}}{4} \times 16 \times 3 = 12\sqrt{3} \text{ cm}^2$

27. Area of equilateral triangle $= \sqrt{3}$ m²

$\frac{\sqrt{3}}{4}a^2 = \sqrt{3}$

$a^2 = 4 \Rightarrow a = 2$ m

36. Perimeter = 480

$2(l + b) = 480$

$2(5x + 3x) = 480$

$\Rightarrow \quad x = \frac{240}{8} = 30$

Area $= l \times b = 150 \times 90$

$= 13500 \text{ m}^2$

43. Diagonal $= \sqrt{l^2 + b^2}$

$17 = \sqrt{l^2 + 8^2}$

$l^2 = 17^2 - 8^2 = 225$

$l = 15$ m

Perimeter $= 2(l + b) = 2(15 + 8)$

= 46 cm

44. $2\pi r = 132$

$2 \times \frac{22}{7} \times r = 132$

$\Rightarrow \quad r = \frac{132 \times 7}{44} = 21$ cm

Area $= \pi r^2 = \frac{22}{7} \times 21^2$

$= \frac{22}{7} \times 21 \times 21 = 1386 \text{ cm}^2$

49. Circumference $= \pi d = \frac{22}{7} \times 7 = 22$ cm

50. Third side = 34 – (12 + 14)

= 34 – 26

= 8 cm

51. Area of circle = 1386

$\pi r^2 = 1386$

$\frac{22}{7} \times r^2 = 1386$

$r^2 = \frac{1386 \times 7}{22} = 441$

$r = \sqrt{441} = 21$ cm

Perimeter of Circle $= 2\pi r = 2 \times \frac{22}{7} \times 21$

$= 132$ cm

52. Side of square = $\sqrt{324} = 18$ m

Diagonal of square = $18\sqrt{2}$ m

53. Breadth $= \frac{960}{48} = 20$ m

Perimeter of rectangle = 2(l + b)

= 2 (48 × 20)

= 2 × 68 = 136 m

Cost of fencing = 136 × 7 = ₹ 952

54. Diagonal of a square = $13\sqrt{2}$ cm

$\sqrt{2} \times \text{side} = 13\sqrt{2}$

Side = 13 cm

Perimeter = 4 × side = 4 × 13 = 52 cm

55. Third side = 56 – (7 + 25) = 56 – 32

= 24 cm

Area of triangle = $\frac{1}{2} \times 7 \times 24 = 84$ cm^2

56. Side of square = $\sqrt{1225} = 35$ m

Perimeter = 4 × side = 4 × 35 = 140 m

57. Perimeter of semi-circle = $\pi r + 2r$

$= \frac{22}{7} \times 28 + 2 \times 28$

= 88 + 56

= 144 cm

58. Length = $\frac{750}{25} = 30$ m

Perimeter of rectangle = 2(l + b)

= 2 (30 + 25)

= 110 m

59. $s = \frac{7+14+15}{2} = \frac{36}{2} = \mathbf{18}$

Area of triangle

$= \sqrt{s(s-a)(s-b)(s-c)}$

$= \sqrt{18(18-7)(18-14)(18-15)}$

$= \sqrt{18 \times 11 \times 4 \times 3}$

$= \sqrt{9 \times 2 \times 11 \times 4 \times 3}$

$= 6\sqrt{66}$ cm^2

60. Area of equilateral triangle = $16\sqrt{3}$

$\frac{\sqrt{3}}{4} \times (\text{side})^2 = 16\sqrt{3}$

Side = $\sqrt{64} = 8$ m

Perimeter = 8 × 3 = 24 m

9. GEOMETRICAL SHAPES AND ANGLES

Answer Key

1. (a)	2. (d)	3. (a)	4. (c)	5. (a)	6. (c)	7. (d)	8. (d)	9. (a)	10. (b)
11. (c)	12. (c)	13. (c)	14. (c)	15. (b)	16. (d)	17. (a)	18. (a)	19. (b)	20. (a)
21. (b)	22. (c)	23. (c)	24. (a)	25. (a)	26. (c)	27. (a)	28. (b)	29. (a)	30. (b)
31. (c)	32. (c)	33. (a)	34. (b)	35. (a)	36. (b)	37. (c)	38. (c)	39. (d)	40. (a)
41. (a)	42. (c)	43. (d)	44. (a)	45. (d)	46. (c)	47. (b)	48. (c)	49. (b)	50. (d)

38. Required angle = $154° - 90° = 64°$

41. Required angle = $360° - 297° = 63°$

LOGICAL REASONING

Answer Key

1. (a)	2. (d)	3. (b)	4. (c)	5. (a)	6. (d)	7. (d)	8. (d)	9. (d)	10. (c)
11. (c)	12. (d)	13. (a)	14. (c)	15. (c)	16. (c)	17. (d)	18. (b)	19. (d)	20. (c)
21. (d)	22. (c)	23. (c)	24. (c)	25. (d)	26. (d)	27. (c)	28. (b)	29. (d)	30. (b)
31. (b)	32. (c)	33. (b)	34. (a)	35. (a)	36. (c)	37. (b)	38. (a)	39. (c)	40. (b)
41. (c)	42. (b)	43. (c)	44. (b)	45. (b)	46. (b)	47. (d)	48. (b)	49. (b)	50. (d)
51. (d)	52. (a)	53. (c)	54. (c)	55. (b)	56. (d)	57. (a)	58. (d)	59. (b)	60. (a)
61. (d)	62. (a)	63. (b)	64. (c)	65. (d)	66. (a)	67. (b)	68. (d)	69. (b)	70. (b)
71. (c)	72. (d)	73. (a)	74. (d)	75. (d)	76. (d)	77. (c)	78. (b)	79. (c)	80. (a)
81. (b)	82. (a)	83. (d)	84. (c)	85. (c)	86. (d)	87. (a)	88. (d)	89. (c)	90. (b)
91. (b)	92. (c)	93. (d)	94. (a)	95. (c)	96. (a)	97. (b)	98. (a)	99. (c)	100. (a)

ACHIEVERS SECTION

Answer Key

1. (c)	2. (d)	3. (b)	4. (d)	5. (d)	6. (a)	7. (b)	8. (b)	9. (a)	10. (c)
11. (b)	12. (d)	13. (d)	14. (b)	15. (b)	16. (a)	17. (c)	18. (d)	19. (c)	20. (c)
21. (a)	22. (d)	23. (b)	24. (b)	25. (d)	26. (c)	27. (a)	28. (a)	29. (b)	30. (a)
31. (b)	32. (b)	33. (d)	34. (b)	35. (b)	36. (b)	37. (d)	38. (a)	39. (d)	40. (d)
41. (a)	42. (b)	43. (a)	44. (a)	45. (b)	46. (b)	47. (a)	48. (c)	49. (a)	50. (a)

1. $\frac{1}{3}$ of $x = 60$

$\Rightarrow x = 60 \times 3 = 180$ litres

$\frac{1}{2} \times 180 = 90$ litres

3. x of $\frac{1}{12} = \frac{3}{8}$

$\Rightarrow x = \frac{3}{8} \times 12 = \frac{9}{2}$

6. $\angle AOB = 180° - 143° = 37°$

7. $90° - 67° = 23°$

12. Number of days = 29

Required number of hours = 29 × 24 = 696

13.

kg	gm
7	50
9	970
+ 12	335
29	355

14.

l	ml
6	1015
− 5	870
1	145

15. 2 hours 15 minutes

= 2 × 60 + 15 = 135 minute

= 135 × 60 = 8100 seconds

16. 7 m 17 cm = (7 × 100 + 17) cm

= 717 cm

717 cm = 717 × 10 = 7170 mm

18. 2000 − (795 + 435 + 295) = 475

19. 65 − 75 ÷ 15 + (14 − 6) + 27

= 65 − 5 + 8 + 27 = 95

20. 137 − (17 + 23) + 150 ÷ 25 − 18

= 137 − 40 + 6 − 18

= 143 − 58 = 85

21. Smallest four digit number = 1000

Largest three digit number = 999

Difference = 1000 − 999 = 1

24. $\frac{1}{8} + \frac{1}{7} + \frac{1}{9}$

$= \frac{63 + 72 + 56}{504} = \frac{191}{504}$

26. $\frac{2}{7} = 0.28$; $\frac{3}{11} = 0.27$

$\frac{7}{12} = 0.58$ $\frac{8}{17} = 0.47$

$\frac{7}{12} > \frac{8}{17} > \frac{2}{7} > \frac{3}{11}$

32. $\frac{\text{LCM of 4, 5, 6}}{\text{HCF of 5, 6, 7}} = \frac{120}{1} = 120$

1. $\frac{1}{3}$ of $x = 60$

$\Rightarrow x = 60 \times 3 = 180$ litres

$\frac{1}{2} \times 180 = 90$ litres

3. x of $\frac{1}{12} = \frac{3}{8}$

$\Rightarrow x = \frac{3}{8} \times 12 = \frac{9}{2}$

6. $\angle AOB = 180° - 143° = 37°$

7. $90° - 67° = 23°$

12. Number of days = 29

Required number of hours = 29 × 24 = 696

13.

	kg	gm
	7	50
	9	970
+	12	335
	29	355

14.

	l	ml
	6	1015
−	5	870
	1	145

15. 2 hours 15 minutes

= 2 × 60 + 15 = 135 minute

= 135 × 60 = 8100 seconds

16. 7 m 17 cm = (7 × 100 + 17) cm

= 717 cm

717 cm = 717 × 10 = 7170 mm

18. 2000 – (795 + 435 + 295) = 475

19. 65 – 75 ÷ 15 + (14 – 6) + 27

= 65 – 5 + 8 + 27 = 95

20. 137 – (17 + 23) + 150 ÷ 25 – 18

= 137 – 40 + 6 – 18

= 143 – 58 = 85

21. Smallest four digit number = 1000

Largest three digit number = 999

Difference = 1000 – 999 = 1

24. $\frac{1}{8} + \frac{1}{7} + \frac{1}{9}$

$= \frac{63 + 72 + 56}{504} = \frac{191}{504}$

26. $\frac{2}{7} = 0.28$; $\frac{3}{11} = 0.27$

$\frac{7}{12} = 0.58$ $\frac{8}{17} = 0.47$

$\frac{7}{12} > \frac{8}{17} > \frac{2}{7} > \frac{3}{11}$

32. $\frac{\text{LCM of 4, 5, 6}}{\text{HCF of 5, 6, 7}} = \frac{120}{1} = 120$

33. Sum = 8732 + 2378 = 11110

34. Difference = 7640 – 4067 = 3573

37. 631 + 1200 ÷ 6 × 2 + 417 × 2

= 631 + 200 × 2 + 417 × 2

= 631 + 400 + 834 = 1865

41. Area $= \pi r^2 = \frac{22}{7} \times 7^2 = 154$ cm²

Circumference $= 2\pi r = 2 \times \frac{22}{7} \times 7 = 44$ cm

45. A : B = 3 : 5 = 6 : 10

B : C = 2 : 3 = 10 : 15

A : B : C = 6 : 10 : 15

48. Dividend = 157 × 308 + 17

= 48373

Printed by Libri Plureos GmbH in Hamburg,
Germany

9 789357 942485